ON THE COVER

APRICOT JAM

Jam According to Daniel
Charlottesville, Virginia

CHEESE

Spring Mill Farm + Caromont Farm
Concord + Charlottesville, Virginia

MEAT + BREAD

Timbercreek Market
Charlottesville, Virginia

RASPBERRIES

Agriberry Farm
Hanover, Virginia

WINE, GRAPES, APPLES + PERSIMMONS

Early Mountain Vineyards
Madison, Virginia

THE VIRGINIA TABLE

PHOTOGRAPHS **ANDREA HUBBELL + SARAH CRAMER SHIELDS** | STORIES **JENNY PAURYS**

A LOVE LETTER TO VIRGINIA

BY JEAN CASE

My husband, Steve, and I have called Virginia home for more than thirty years, from our days building a then-unknown startup called America Online, to raising a family, to our current role as investors in local businesses and nonprofit organizations. Over the years, we have watched with delight as Virginia has become a jewel of the South, with visitors and residents alike discovering all the gifts it has to offer.

The country has fallen in love with Virginia, in no small part because of our world-class wine, top-ranked chefs and restaurants, flourishing farms, and outstanding artisanal foods. One need only catch a glimpse of a farmers' market on a Saturday morning to understand: there is a movement afoot in our great state.

This book is something we've wanted to create for some time, and we're delighted that we found the talented storytellers at Our Local Commons to bring this vision to life. *The Virginia Table* is our way of capturing a snapshot of what is coming to life in our own backyard. To do it, we're sharing the perspectives of celebrated champions within the Virginia food and wine industry, like Chef José Andrés of ThinkFoodGroup, Michael Babin of Neighborhood Restaurant Group, and Dave McIntyre of *The Washington Post*—individuals who have lifted the Commonwealth's profile through their dedication to their craft and their support and enthusiasm for our farmers, food artisans, and winemakers.

We are also excited to shine a spotlight on the next generation of women and men who are taking Virginia to a new level of food and wine recognition. These young, up-and-coming artisans deserve our full attention, and we are thrilled to share their stories in the pages of this book.

Taken as whole, *The Virginia Table* reflects the strong foundation of Virginia's current epicurean scene and illustrates the energy, passion, and devotion that is fueling innovation and pushing Virginia to the forefront of America's "go local" movement.

When we started Early Mountain Vineyards, we committed to showcasing the best of what Virginia had to offer. We served not just our own wines, but high-quality varietals from all over the Commonwealth. In that same spirit, we want to continue telling a larger story about the best of what's happening in the many areas that make up the Virginia table—from cheese and wine, to grains and beer, to meat and cider.

When I look at what has transpired here in Virginia over the past three decades, I feel extremely proud. It is a view of the Commonwealth that I am delighted to share with you. Enjoy!

Sincerely,

APPLES
CARTER MOUNTAIN ORCHARD
CHARLOTTESVILLE, VIRGINIA

GRAPES
VERITAS VINEYARD AND WINERY
AFTON, VIRGINIA

HOPS
BLUE MOUNTAIN BREWERY
AFTON, VIRGINIA

ROAST + HERBS
TIMBERCREEK MARKET
CHARLOTTESVILLE, VIRGINIA

WHOLE-WHEAT FLOUR
WOODSON'S MILL
LOWESVILLE, VIRGINIA

TABLE OF CONTENTS

FOREWORD 5
*A Love Letter to Virginia
by Jean Case*

PATRICK EVANS-HYLTON . . .10
Tastemaker

MEAT

JM STOCK PROVISIONS 12
Artisan Profile

VA BUTCHERS 16
Made in Virginia

BROOKVILLE 18
Recipes + Pairings

KENDRA FEATHER 20
Tastemaker

CIDER

BLUE BEE CIDER 22
Artisan Profile

VA'S VARIED CIDERS 26
Made in Virginia

FORAGE 28
Recipes + Pairings

MICHAEL BABIN 32
Tastemaker

CHEESE

SPRING MILL FARM 34
Artisan Profile

**CHEESEMONGER'S
VA CHOICE** 38
Made in Virginia

PASTURE 40
Recipes + Pairings

DAVE MCINTYRE 42
Tastemaker

WINE

**EARLY MOUNTAIN
VINEYARDS** 44
Artisan Profile

12 VA GEMS 48
Made in Virginia

ROCKSALT 50
Recipes + Pairings

JOSÉ ANDRÉS 52
Tastemaker

GRAIN

STEADFAST FARM 54
Artisan Profile

GRAINS FROM VA 58
Made in Virginia

THE RED HEN 60
Recipes + Pairings

TARVER KING 62
Tastemaker

BEER

**THREE NOTCH'D
BREWING COMPANY** 64
Artisan Profile

BEER RUN'S VA PICKS 68
Made in Virginia

THE SHACK 70
Recipes + Pairings

NEAL + STAR WAVRA 72
Tastemakers

AFTERWORD 77
by Our Local Commons

ACKNOWLEDGEMENTS 78

"Not only can Virginia feed herself, indeed historically all of her citizens ate locally and ate well. We need to replace the impression of natural, nutrient-dense, artisanal food being solely the purview of the well-heeled with a vision of a sustainable local agri-economy that can nourish all of Virginia's citizens."

— JOHN WHITESIDE, OWNER + FARMER
WOLF CREEK FARM
GRASS-FED, GRASS-FINISHED BEEF
MADISON COUNTY, VIRGINIA

FOOD WRITER, EDITOR + COLUMNIST | **INFO / PATRICKEVANSHYLTON.COM**

On a visit to southwestern Virginia two years ago, Patrick Evans-Hylton had the opportunity to interview renowned bluegrass artist Dr. Ralph Stanley, a native of the area. Recognizing that journalists have likely asked Dr. Stanley every question in the book, Patrick decided to approach their discussion from his own area of expertise: food culture.

"Dr. Stanley," he asked, "can you tell me a dish that your mother made that you wish you could have again?" Dr. Stanley's eyes brightened, and he launched into a vivid recollection of his mother's homemade country ham.

This connection between people, food, places, and time is at the heart of Patrick's lifetime interest in food culture and heritage. "I think that's the most beautiful thing about food," he says. "It really is a time machine. Whether it's somebody that's passed, or you're just thinking about a great experience that you've had—those memories can be passed along, too."

Patrick's own desire for authentic food was shaped by his grandmother, who raised him from infancy. "She was always in the kitchen, and I was always there with her," he says. That connection stayed with Patrick, and he began to immerse himself in learning, teaching, and writing about the culinary traditions of Virginia and the South, a career that now spans more than a dozen books and a host of local and regional newspapers and magazines, for which he serves as a columnist and editor. Over time, he has observed Virginia's ascension from a state with a culinary inferiority complex to one that was named by *Esquire* as the Food Region of 2014. It's a transformation linked to a collective, nationwide search for identity, galvanized, he feels, after September 11, 2001.

"We started naturally thinking about our childhood, our growing up, our parents, our grandparents," he says. "We're returning to that, and we're settling into our own special type of American cuisine."

The roots of the nation's culinary identity originated here in the Commonwealth, Patrick says. "You trace back all of the major American foodways, and they all started here in Virginia," he explains, a line that extends back to the first settlers, who in order to survive had to utilize ingredients native to America and its indigenous cultures. The subsequent influx of enslaved laborers added Afro-Caribbean elements to this nascent foodscape. While these were uncomfortable cultural unions—and remain so to this day—the resulting cuisine proved to be better than the sum of its parts.

> "You trace back all of the major American foodways, and they all started here in Virginia."

Today, those foundations are finding new vibrancy in the hands of talented Virginia chefs, many of whom take great pride in anchoring their craft in the bounty of ingredients raised, grown, and handcrafted in the Commonwealth. "We still have our wonderful signature dishes—what I like to call our culinary calling cards—but we're really creating a new Virginia cuisine," Patrick says. "I've seen it in Abingdon. I've seen it in Roanoke. I've seen it in Staunton and Harrisonburg, Northern Virginia, Richmond, coastal Virginia, and Charlottesville—it's happening everywhere. It really is. And it's happening because it's real food."

Patrick and his grandmother remained very close throughout his adult life. She died two years ago, and when he's asked about the one dish she made that he wishes he could have again, his answer harkens back to her kitchen.

"Just some biscuits and butter," he replies. "It was just such an intimate act, to make those biscuits with her arthritic hands. She never measured anything, and she pat down the top of the biscuits in the little round pan." He grins, dimples forming on his cheeks, his mind conjuring some moment that only the two of them knew.

"It's almost like you could taste the love." ●

JM STOCK PROVISIONS

OWNERS + BUTCHERS / **MATTHEW GREENE + JAMES LUM III** | CITY / **CHARLOTTESVILLE** | INFO / **STOCKPROVISIONS.COM**

The slight creak of the front door at JM Stock Provisions announces the arrival of customers and purveyors, and on this Tuesday morning, its clamor is constant. Outside, the weekday is swinging into full motion, with cars filling up the parking spots on either side of West Main Street in Midtown Charlottesville—an old neighborhood that links the city's historic Downtown Mall to the University of Virginia. All morning long, locals stream into the butcher shop, nabbing ham biscuits and coffee, or picking up a cut of meat, a selection of sausages, or a pound of bacon.

Behind the counter, the activity is equally energetic. A motorized sausage mixer hums as two of the shop's butchers feed spiced ground pork through the cylinder into the sausage casing. The shop stocks about six of its many sausage varieties on any given day, from Red Wine & Rosemary to Ginger & Scallion to Andouille. The team has just finished a batch when farmer John Whiteside walks in.

It's delivery day for John, who owns Wolf Creek Farm in Madison County, where he raises grass-fed, grass-finished beef. He is delivering beef quarters, and the JM Stock crew heads out to the delivery van to help carry them in, hoisting the meat onto the shop's butcher block counters. The quarters are immense, but no sooner have they been set on the counter then the butchers are unwrapping them and breaking them down. It's all hands on deck, and the shop's owners, Matthew Greene and James Lum III, are in the thick of it, expertly dividing the cuts. They are impressed with the quality of the product, a testimony to the farmer who raised it.

"John Whiteside is a really amazing man," James says, stepping back from the workbench.

Matt nods in agreement. "He produces great product," he says.

Today's delivery is the result of more than a year of relationship-building for Matt and James, who first approached John with an interest in carrying his farm's beef at the shop. John's response wasn't what you might expect: he told them he'd be happy to sell to them, but it would take a year to carefully grow the herd in order to accommodate their needs. In some ways, that is exactly the kind of answer Matt and James wanted to hear.

"He was really straightforward with us," Matt says. "He didn't bend over backwards to snatch up our business, and he didn't make any compromises to the business model he already has."

Matt explains that much about Wolf Creek Farm impresses him: the manner in which the animals are raised, fed, and cared for, for starters, which has led to Wolf Creek Farm's certification as Animal Welfare Approved—the only beef producer in Virginia with that distinction. Matt also respects John's approach to business and his dedication to an intentionally diverse customer base, instead of just a few large clients, allowing room for an up-and-coming butcher shop such as JM Stock.

James and Matt have had the same experience with other local meat producers—Autumn Olive Farms near Waynesboro, Deep Rock Farm in White Hall, and River Oak Farm in Lowesville. In every case, James and Matt's interest was greeted with enthusiasm, balanced by the farmers' focus on the careful management of their animals.

"I love that about where we are right now," James says, "being able to support a lot of different farmers."

This hands-on involvement with the products they carry in the shop—visiting farms, interacting face-to-face with the farmers—is a part of their business that James and Matt relish. They conceptualized JM Stock after working at a butcher shop in Brooklyn, New York. Both were interested in returning to their native Virginia, but they wanted to continue working with nose-to-tail butchery practices, which emphasize the quality of the animal's life, its humane slaughter, and using every part of it through careful butchery techniques.

Charlottesville, with its enthusiasm for farm-to-table, seemed like an ideal fit for the kind of shop Matt and James envisioned. They found an old storefront on West Main Street, renovated it to suit their needs, and opened shop in October 2013. While JM Stock was an instant favorite among local foodies, it took some time to gain the customer base James and Matt were seeking.

"What's the phrase?" Matt asks, jokingly. "Overnight success takes about fifteen years?"

And yet, little by little, JM Stock gained its footing and a solid following in the community. That success, in turn, led to another challenge: maintaining a steady supply of inventory. Matt and James know what they are looking for in the meat they carry in the store, and they are uncompromising in that commitment to quality. The animals must be raised well and cared for, given the

> "I want to support the guy who wants to do it because he loves to do it, because he's passionate about doing it the right way—which is generally the hard way."

best conditions available in which to eat and live, and slaughtered with care and respect—all factors integral to the caliber of the final product.

"One thing that's been interesting for us is our increase in production has affected the way we buy products," James explains. "A lot of the farmers we work with are small farmers. That's great. I want to support the guy who wants to do it because he loves to do it, because he's passionate about doing it the right way—which is generally the hard way. But, that being said, as we grow, we sometimes outgrow the farm. Which gives us more work. It's fun work and the kind of work that Matt and I like: going to visit new producers and meeting new farmers and realizing there's more than just a handful of people doing the right thing out there."

"We try to market ourselves as a sort of connoisseur," Matt adds. "We curate the store with the best possible farms that we can source from."

With the relationship-building part of their business starting to bear fruit, Matt and James are beginning to see their vision come to fruition. They are looking to utilize the sturdy foundation they've built over the past two years to usher their business into a new era—one in which it is an indelible part of Charlottesville's robust food culture.

New avenues for growth are presenting themselves as well. In the summer of 2015, James moved to Richmond, where he will focus on further building out the shop's satellite meat counter at Harvest Grocery, in the city's Fan District, a venture they launched in 2014. James is thrilled to be there amid Richmond's burgeoning restaurant scene.

"Seeing new great stuff open up gives me a kind of satisfaction," he says. "We may not have the plethora of options that New York, or San Francisco or Atlanta have, but the stuff we have is great. And it's growing. It's already grown."

Here in Midtown Charlottesville, foot traffic is picking up at the butcher counter as morning gives way to the lunchtime rush. The beef quarters are already broken down, the beautifully marbled meat finding a spot in the walk-in cooler or the shop's front case. Matt and James tie their aprons on, and get back to work. ●

WOLF CREEK FARM

OWNER + FARMER / **JOHN WHITESIDE**
INFO / **WOLFCREEKFARM.COM**

At Wolf Creek Farm in Madison, Virginia, John Whiteside raises grass-fed, grass-finished beef cattle the best way he knows how—from the ground up.

"We start with the land and the soil," says John, explaining that Wolf Creek uses no chemicals, pesticides, or herbicides in its pastures, and a mix of grasses attuned to warm and cool seasons provide year-round grazing for its 600 head of cattle. Even the water originates from within the farm and is carefully protected from contamination.

Wolf Creek's commitment to sustainability even extends to its immediate community, where everyone who works on the farm lives, and where Wolf Creek sources the materials needed for its infrastructure. From there, the farm's sustainability mission expands to its customer base. "All of our product is sold and consumed here locally, which completes the cycle of keeping the business—the operation of the farm—totally sustainable," John says, noting that all of Wolf Creek's sales are made directly to the consumer or through its partnerships with locally owned retailers.

John believes the Commonwealth is ideal for Wolf Creek's sustainable beef model. "Virginia has always been great cattle country," he says, emphasizing the quality of the state's water, soils, and grasses. "We still have that heritage here, and we still have a lot of the old-school ability to raise animals naturally."

VA BUTCHERS

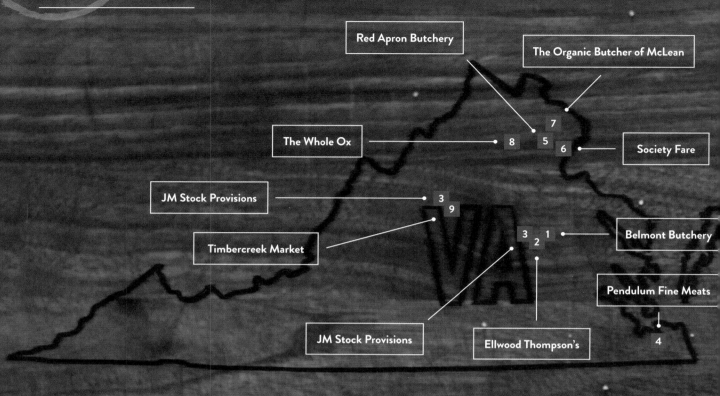

Red Apron Butchery

The Organic Butcher of McLean

The Whole Ox

Society Fare

JM Stock Provisions

Timbercreek Market

Belmont Butchery

Pendulum Fine Meats

JM Stock Provisions

Ellwood Thompson's

1. Belmont Butchery
Richmond, Virginia
belmontbutchery.com

Look for: Pastured lamb from Tuckahoe Lamb and Cattle Company in Cartersville, Virginia

2. Ellwood Thompson's
Richmond, Virginia
ellwoodthompsons.com

Look for: Ribeyes and New York strips from Buffalo Creek Beef in Lexington, Virginia

3. JM Stock Provisions
Charlottesville + Richmond, Virginia
stockprovisions.com

Look for: 60 rotating varieties of housemade sausage featuring pork from Autumn Olive Farms in

4. Pendulum Fine Meats
Norfolk, Virginia
pendulummeats.com

Look for: Grass-fed beef from River Road Farm in Franklin, Virginia

5. Red Apron Butchery
Fairfax, Virginia
redapronbutchery.com

Look for: Smoked fennel sausage made from Russaback pork, a Russian boar crossed with a Saddleback, from Leaping Waters Farm in Alleghany Springs, Virginia

6. Society Fare
Alexandria, Virginia
societyfair.net

Look for: Rose veal from Chapel Hill Farm in Berryville, Virginia

7. The Organic Butcher of McLean
McLean, Virginia
theorganicbutcherofmclean.com

Look for: Freshly ground, certified organic grass-fed beef from Mount Airy Farms in Upperville, Virginia

8. The Whole Ox
Marshall, Virginia
thewholeox.com

Look for: Pastured chicken from Yohanan Farm in Purcellville, Virginia

9. Timbercreek Market
Charlottesville, Virginia
timbercreekmarket.com

Look for: Housemade prosciutto from pork raised at Timbercreek Farm in Albemarle County,

GRASS-FED, GRASS-FINISHED BEEF
TIMBERCREEK MARKET
CHARLOTTESVILLE, VIRGINIA

KNIFE BY
MONOLITH STUDIO
IVY, VIRGINIA

RECEIPES + PAIRINGS | BROOKVILLE

RECIPES / **HARRISON + JENNIFER KEEVIL** | RESTAURANT / **BROOKVILLE RESTAURANT** | LOCATION / **CHARLOTTESVILLE** | INFO / **BROOKVILLERESTAURANT.COM**

COUNTRY HAM BISCUITS

Nothing is more Southern than baking powder biscuits—except baking powder biscuits stuffed with country ham. Chef Harrison Keevil—co-owner with his wife, Jennifer, of Brookville Restaurant in Charlottesville—likes to use ham from Timbercreek Farm in Albemarle County, which partners with Kite's Hams in Madison County to cure its country ham. Chef Keevil serves these biscuits with another Southern staple, pepper jelly.

Makes about a dozen biscuits.

- **3 cups all-purpose flour**
- **2 Tbsp. baking powder**
- **1 ½ tsp. salt**
- **½ pound (2 sticks) cold, unsalted butter**
- **1 ½ cups milk**
- **Country ham, thinly sliced**
- **Pepper jelly (recipe follows)**

Preheat oven to 400 degrees.

Combine the flour, baking powder, and salt into a large bowl. Using the largest holes of a box grater, grate the cold butter into the flour mixture, then rub the mixture between your hands to evenly distribute the butter into the flour. Add all the milk, stirring until everything is moistened.

Turn the dough out onto a lightly floured work surface and pack it together to form a ball. Pat it down and fold it in half over itself, then give it a quarter turn and pat it down into about ¾-inch thickness and fold it in half. Repeat the turn-pat-and-fold 4 more times.

Using a bench scraper or knife, cut out biscuits into 3-by-3-inch squares and place them an inch apart on a baking sheet. Bake until golden brown, about 18 minutes. Split biscuits and stuff with pepper jelly and slices of ham.

JEN PEN'S PEPPER JELLY

Note from Jennifer: This recipe changes a smidge throughout the summer depending on what the garden is growing and what I harvest each time I make the jelly. Be sure to use a total of 5 cups of peppers. (The amounts given for the whole peppers are estimates—it will depend on the size of your peppers.)

I let my jars sit anywhere between three and four weeks to allow the flavor to develop and the jelly to gain a nice texture. My dad always served his pepper jelly over a log of cream cheese, and we would eat it on Ritz Crackers. Nowadays, we eat this jelly on just about everything—but my favorite is still cream cheese and Ritz Crackers!

Makes 6 half-pint jars.

- **3 cups finely diced banana peppers (about a dozen whole)**
- **1 cup finely diced jalapeño peppers (15 to 20 whole)**
- **¼ cup finely diced habanero peppers (15 to 20 whole)**
- **¼ cup finely diced bell peppers (2 to 3 whole)**
- **¼ cup finely diced hot lemon peppers (about a dozen whole)**
- **¼ cup finely diced ghost peppers (4 to 5 whole)**
- **1 cup apple cider vinegar**
- **1 ¾ oz. powdered fruit pectin**
- **5 cups granulated sugar**

Sterilize six 8-ounce canning jars and lids according to the manufacturer's instructions.

Place the diced peppers in a large saucepan over high heat. Add the vinegar and pectin and combine. Stirring constantly, bring the mixture to a full and rolling boil. Add all the sugar and stir until the sugar is completely dissolved. Return to a full boil, and boil exactly 1 minute. Remove the pan from the heat and skim off any foam.

Quickly ladle the mixture into jars, filling to within ¼ inch of the rim. Wipe the rims with a clean, damp cloth or paper towel. Cover the jars with the lids and screw on the metal bands firmly.

To process, fill a water bath canner and heat until the water is hot but not boiling. Slowly lower the jars onto the canner rack. The water should cover the jars completely. Bring the water to a boil and process for exactly 5 minutes. Remove the jars from the water and let cool on a rack or towel.

Check the seals on the cooled jars by pressing down in the center of each lid. If the lid is depressed and does not move when pressed, the jar is sealed. Unsealed jars should be stored in the refrigerator and the jelly used within a few days.

Harrison Keevil
Chef + co-Owner
Brookville Restaurant

TASTEMAKER | KENDRA FEATHER

FOUNDER / IPANEMA CAFE, GARNETT'S CAFE, THE ROOSEVELT + WPA BAKERY | INFO / ROOSEVELTRVA.COM

In 2011, Kendra Feather was given an opportunity: to breathe new life into a defunct restaurant at the corner of North 25th Street and M Street in the Church Hill neighborhood of Richmond, an area that at the time had few successful eateries. The early 1900s building was in foreclosure when Kendra discovered it, but she believed it offered a lot of promise—if she could figure out the right restaurant for it.

> "You want to live in a place where you can walk down the street to your local coffee shop. It doesn't have to be anything fancy—it just has to be yours."

"Some people have a concept and go seek out a place to put it in," Kendra says. "I've always done it the other way around. I'm an accidental restaurateur—I don't know how else to explain it. I stumble across opportunities."

The opportunity Kendra stumbled across became The Roosevelt, a 50-seat restaurant she co-owns with Chef Lee Gregory, a James Beard Foundation Award nominee, offering Southern-inspired fare, an all-Virginia wine list, and a wealth of local and regional beers. It quickly became a critical success, heralded as a shining light in Church Hill. For Kendra—a self-made businesswoman who turned a college job waiting tables into a small restaurant empire in Richmond that also includes two restaurants in the city's Fan District and a bakery in Church Hill—the neighborhood is always a crucial part of that success.

"You become part of the fabric of people's lives over time," Kendra says, recalling couples, now married, who had their first dates at The Roosevelt, and families who brought in their babies after the restaurant opened—children who are now school-age. "Restaurants add to the vibrancy of a neighborhood."

Church Hill traces its history to the very founding of Richmond and has played an equally auspicious role in the history of Virginia: it was here in 1775, at St. John's Church on East Broad Street, that Patrick Henry proclaimed, "Give me liberty, or give me death!" But its proud heritage was not enough to ensure Church Hill's long-term vitality, and in the second half of the twentieth century, as families left the city for the suburbs, much of the neighborhood fell into disrepair. Now it is undergoing a transformation, with new residents and homegrown businesses, like The Roosevelt, moving in. Kendra, who also lives in Church Hill, sees this metamorphosis as part of a broader shift taking place across Virginia, and the entire United States, with Richmond serving as a proud example of the possibilities of urban restoration.

"People are going back to cities," she observes. "You want to live in a place where you can walk down the street to your local coffee shop. It doesn't have to be anything fancy—it just has to be yours."

Kendra calls this "home team pride"—a feeling that is helping bring places like Church Hill, with its rich, complex history, into a new era: one where residents embrace local businesses and, in turn, see the neighborhoods around them flourish.

"People are realizing that they can have a home team everywhere," Kendra says. ●

BLUE BEE CIDER

CIDERY FOUNDER + OWNER / **COURTNEY MAILEY** | CITY / **RICHMOND** | INFO / **BLUEBEECIDER.COM**

Midday on a summer Monday, a small group of visitors arrives at the Blue Bee Cider tasting room in the Old Manchester industrial neighborhood of downtown Richmond. Tucked in a 1900s brick building, the room is comfortable and cozy, with a simple bar for tastings. A wall behind the bar showcases an array of bottles, all carrying the Blue Bee label. Eight flagship artisanal ciders are made and bottled here, as well as many other small-batch ciders that are available on tap.

Standing behind the bar, Courtney Mailey greets the group as it arrives. As owner and founder of Blue Bee Cider, manning the tasting room is just one of a stack of hats Courtney wears. This urban cidery—the first of its kind in Virginia when it opened in 2013—is the culmination of fifteen years of dreams, plans, and careful execution, and the realization of a desire that echoes back to Courtney's early childhood: maintaining a connection to nature. "My mom never had to tell me to go play outside," she says. Later, in high school, the results of an aptitude test surprised her.

"Everyone in my class was 'doctor,' 'lawyer,' 'engineer,' 'architect,'" Courtney recalls. "I was 'farmer.' I thought, 'What's going on? This test is wrong.'"

After college, Courtney took a desk job in economic development in Washington, D.C., but quickly saw that it didn't jibe with her love of the outdoors. "I just wanted to be outside, and I don't know why I thought just because I was educated, I would suddenly sit at a desk and be happy," she says. She continued to build a career in economic development but never got used to working in an office building, and she found herself thinking back to that high school aptitude test. "I started to realize, 'Maybe that test was right,'" she recalls. "And I started to give agriculture a real thought."

With Virginia's wealth of established apple orchards and strong tradition of apple growing, Courtney saw significant potential in cider—an age-old alcoholic craft beverage enjoying a meaningful resurgence, both in the Commonwealth and throughout the United States. After painstaking planning, in December 2010 she made the leap, enrolling in a two-week cidermaking

"You have to be brilliant to make it in agriculture. The margins are teeny-tiny."

program at Cornell University, in tandem with her father, Mel Anderson, who had also been bitten by the cidermaking bug. "I quit my job on Friday," she says. "I went to cider school on Saturday." Mel drove them, attended the course with her, and eventually helped her get the cidery off the ground—a shared project that has deepened their connection. You can now find him behind the tasting room bar one day a week, his enthusiasm for the cidery—and his daughter—wholly apparent.

Courtney went on to complete a one-year apprenticeship at Albemarle CiderWorks in North Garden, Virginia, and as she built the foundation of skills needed for her craft, she began mulling the idea of an urban cidery right in Virginia's capital. It would be one of only a few in the U.S., and to do it, she would have to overcome the tactical challenge of transporting the apples from orchards she leased in central and western Virginia to a cidery in the heart of Richmond.

"I had to completely rethink the production process because it's different," she says. "The vast majority of my apples are from west of here, and so getting them from there to here and then when

they're here, how to use them before they turn to mush—I had to figure all of that out from scratch." But figure it out she did. She found the warehouse that Blue Bee now calls home, which included a 10-by-240-foot strip of land perfect for fourteen apple trees, the small on-site orchard that Courtney's inner farmer required.

Blue Bee crushed its first apples in October 2012, a process that carried on through the winter before pivoting to bottling, and then to getting ready to open the tasting room in July 2013. It was exhausting, and something Courtney says she couldn't have weathered without Matthew Mateo, her first part-time employee (who went on to become assistant cidermaker before heading off to grad school). "He is the real reason I survived the first harvest year," she says. Courtney also credits Blue Bee's early success to Brian Ahnmarkher, who is her longest-tenured employee. Brian explains that three years ago, an interest in craft beverage drew him to a job pressing apples at the cidery. "She was looking for people to start on the absolute bottom rung," he recalls. "And that's exactly what I wanted, because I knew then I would be part of the process of creating a product." Brian is now the head of sales for the cidery. "Even though I'm a salesman, that's not what it feels like," he says. "It feels like I'm sharing something that we made."

Blue Bee's cidermaker, Manuel Garcia, also got his start in the trenches, beginning on the apple sorting line in February 2013. "I remember him being very careful and wanting to do things right," Courtney says. "He's just continued to prove himself. He's had a pretty fast journey in a short amount of time because he's very dedicated."

As cidermaker, Manuel has helped develop a creative engine for Blue Bee: the cidery's small-batch program, which features ciders crafted in 5- to 50-gallon batches, allowing trials of new blends, yeast strains, and techniques. Many of these small-batch ciders find their way to the tasting room. "If we get a good response, then we know the following year we can expand on it," Manuel explains. Other times, the team uses what they learn from the process of making a particular small batch to inform how they approach other ciders down the road. For example, the team is working on a new small-batch rosé cider that will use berries in the fermentation process, further evolving Blue Bee flagship cider Fanfare, which is a popular rosé created through the infusion of foraged wild mulberries that lend the cider its rosy color and apricot finish.

Small-batch ciders can also end up being bottled, which was the case for a smoked cider, nicknamed Smokestack. Sam Pillow, the cidery's cellar assistant, oversaw the smoking of the apples, and the resulting cider remains near and dear to his heart. "When that one came out, he had all kinds of love for that cider because it was something that he created that was kind of crazy, but people loved it," Manuel says. "Anytime that happens, it's a special moment. Everybody here has one of those." Courtney says her proudest moments have been when they've seen risks pay off, but every success has required a hefty dose of effort and care. "You have to be brilliant to make it in agriculture," she says. "The margins are teeny-tiny."

Blue Bee crafted 3,000 cases of cider in 2014, and as the cidery delves into its 2015 pressing, Courtney is focused on widening its reach. "The first year and a half, all of our sales were within twenty minutes of the front door," she says. "So, getting our arms around being a wider distributer, though still self-distributing—we're still trying to figure all of that out."

"That's the hardest part," she adds. "Figuring out how to figure it out." •

FOGGY RIDGE CIDER

OWNER AND FOUNDER / **DIANE FLYNT**
INFO / **FOGGYRIDGECIDER.COM**

The blossoming of Virginia's artisanal cider industry represents the resurgence of a craft beverage tradition that was pivotal to early Americans. With new generations discovering cider's appeal, Virginia—with its ideal apple-growing terrain and rich orchard heritage—is at the forefront of the revival.

Diane Flynt has led this revolution for nearly two decades, ever since establishing a cider apple orchard in Dugspur, Virginia, in 1997. In researching cideries, she traveled to England and France and quickly realized that cidermaking was, at its heart, a craft rooted in locality.

"We thought, 'We can come up with an *American* cider, a *Southern* cider—a cider that's right for *this* place,'" Diane recalls. "And that's what we decided to do."

At Foggy Ridge Cider, Diane makes a half-dozen ciders using Virginia-grown cider apples, including rare tannic varieties such as Tremlett's Bitter, Harrison, and Hewe's Crab. Diane has been nominated for a James Beard Foundation award for her work at Foggy Ridge, which is the most widely distributed artisanal cider in the South.

Virginia now boasts more than a dozen cideries, with just as many approaches to making cider. Diane remains proud to be a grower-producer, crafting a product that meets her own high standards. "We wanted to make fabulous cider," she says. "I think we've achieved that."

VA'S VARIED CIDERS

Albemarle CiderWorks
North Garden, Virginia
Look for: Jupiter's Legacy

Blue Bee Cider
Richmond, Virginia
Look for: Mill Race Bramble

Bold Rock Hard Cider
Nellysford, Virginia
Look for: Virginia Apple

Castle Hill
Keswick, Virginia
Look for: Big Pippin

Cobbler Mountain Cellars
Delaplane, Virginia
Look for: Hop Hard Cider

Foggy Ridge Cider
Dugspur, Virginia
Look for: Serious Cider

Old Hill Cider
Timberville, Virginia
Look for: Cidermaker's Barrel

Potter's Craft Cider
Free Union, Virginia
Look for: Hop Cider

Winchester Ciderworks
Winchester, Virginia
Look for: Wicked Wiles Barrel Reserve

ADDITIONAL
VIRGINIA CIDERIES

Blue Toad Hard Cider
Wintergreen, Virginia

Buskey Cider
Richmond, Virginia

**Corcoran Vineyards
and Cidery**
Waterford, Virginia

**Mt. Defiance
Cidery & Distillery**
Middleburg, Virginia

Wild Hare Cider
Bluemont, Virginia

CIDERIES LISTED IN
ALPHABETICAL ORDER

GLASSES FROM **ROXIE DAISY** / CHARLOTTESVILLE, VIRGINIA

RECIPES + PAIRINGS | FORAGE

RECIPES / **MEGAN KIERNAN + JUSTIN STONE** | DINNER SERIES / **FORAGE** | LOCATION / **CHARLOTTESVILLE**

Costume party meets farm-to-table dinner—that is the concept behind Forage, a seasonal dinner series held near Charlottesville. Each dinner features a theme that informs the décor and the menu, and guests are encouraged to participate in their attire, as well. Past iterations have included Hemingway's Paris, 1950s Cleavers' Cookout, and Black & White Masquerade.

These are cozy events, with twenty to thirty guests at each meal, allowing ample opportunity to mingle and converse. The incredibly delicious—and equally creative—meals are created by Megan Kiernan, chef of the café at Feast! in Charlottesville. Megan cofounded Forage in 2012 with Justin Stone, who designs cocktails for each dinner using Charlottesville's own Potter's Craft Cider. Kate Lynn Nemett, who traces her friendship with Megan back to high school drama class, partners with her in the careful creation and orchestration of each event, including writing the official announcement of the dinners, which are sent out to the Forage email list and are just as creatively crafted as the menus.

Forage takes its name from Megan's love of foraging, a time-honored tradition that has enriched meals the world-over for all of human history. No matter the theme, every meal includes at least one foraged ingredient, allowing Megan to share her passion for found ingredients with her guests.

For its autumn 2015 iteration, Forage will host a dinner entitled Arabian Nights. Because many of the Arabian Nights stories begin with "The Story of," that phrasing will be reflected in the menu, and Megan shares one of the dishes here so you, too, can find yourself transported to a distant land.

ROASTED POTATOES WITH LABNEH AND CASTELVETRANO OLIVES

THE STORY OF THE OLIVE AND THE POTATO

Note from the Chef: I tend to prefer to make everything from scratch, and this appetizer, when made as described, is a fantastic composition of textures and flavors. But you can take shortcuts here and still come up with a delicious dish.

Named for the town in Sicily where they're grown, Castelvetrano olives are worth seeking out for their vivid green color and mild, buttery taste. Labneh, a cheese made from yogurt, is available at many Middle Eastern and gourmet markets. You can substitute goat cheese. Leftover labneh will keep for a week in your fridge—it's delicious on almost everything! Or you can roll it into balls, cover it with olive oil, and store in the fridge for up to three weeks. Store-bought roasted red peppers can also be used here.

Note: If you plan on making your own labneh, begin this recipe three days in advance to give it ample time to drain.

Yield: 6 servings

- **Labneh (recipe follows)**
- **1 red bell pepper**
- **4 small red potatoes, sliced a bit less than ¼-inch thick**
- **2 Tbsp. olive oil**
- **1 tsp. salt**
- **Few pinches black pepper**
- **4 oz. Castelvetrano olives, pitted (a cherry pitter works well here)**

LABNEH

- **2 cups plain yogurt**
- **¼ Tbsp. extra-virgin olive oil**
- **2 cloves garlic, smashed**
- **2 tsp. salt**
- **Cheesecloth**
- **Kitchen twine**

To make labneh: Mix yogurt, oil, garlic, and salt in a bowl. Line another, smaller bowl with a double layer of cheesecloth. Scrape yogurt mix into the center of the cloth. Tie two of the corners together at the middle. Place a strip of twine over the knot, and tie the other two corners together securing the twine between the two knots in the center. Hang from a rack in your refrigerator with a bowl below it to catch the draining liquid. The labneh will thicken with time and should be fairly firm within three days.

To roast and peel pepper: If you have a gas stove, roast pepper directly over the flame, turning it with tongs until blackened on both sides. If you have an electric stove, preheat broiler to high. Place pepper on a rimmed baking sheet and broil, flipping it every 5 minutes until both sides are blackened. Enclose pepper for 5 minutes in a paper bag to steam and loosen peel. Slip off skin, remove seeds, and cut pepper into small dice.

Preheat the oven to 425 degrees.

Toss sliced potatoes in a bowl with olive oil, salt, and pepper. Place in a single layer on a baking sheet. Pour any oil remaining in the bowl over the potatoes and bake for 12 minutes. Remove from oven, and with a metal spatula carefully flip potatoes. Bake for another 12 minutes, then check to see if potatoes are crispy and browned on both sides. If not, cook 5 minutes longer.

To assemble: Spread labneh across each of the potato slices. Add a small spoonful of diced roasted red pepper. Top with a pitted olive and serve.

CIDER COCKTAIL

THE STORY OF THE CIDER THIEF

Justin creates his own pomegranate and plum molasses, though commercial varieties of these are also available.

- **2 oz. Potter's Craft Cider**
- **1 oz. apricot-infused brandy**
- **1 oz. pomegranate and plum molasses**
- **A sprig of mint**

To prepare: Pour the brandy and molasses in a shaker with ice, add the mint, and shake. In a rocks glass or cup, pour the cider over an ice cube. Add the contents of the shaker to the glass and garnish with mint.

Megan Kiernan
Chef + Cofounder
Forage

TASTEMAKER | MICHAEL BABIN

CHAIRMAN / **ARCADIA CENTER FOR SUSTAINABLE FOOD & AGRICULTURE**
CAREER / **FOUNDER + MANAGING MEMBER, NEIGHBORHOOD RESTAURANT GROUP**   INFO / **ARCADIAFOOD.ORG**

The dew is heavy on the grass at Arcadia Farm on a sunny summer Monday as the staff prepares for the first day of Small Chefs Farm Camp. One of five weeklong farm camps offered at Arcadia, Small Chefs gives school-aged children from the Washington, D.C., area an opportunity to harvest, wash, prepare, and taste a wealth of vegetables grown at the two-acre farm, located at the historic Woodlawn property in Alexandria, a site of the National Trust for Historic Preservation.

These summer camps are one of Michael Babin's favorite aspects of the Arcadia Center for Sustainable Food & Agriculture, a nonprofit organization his company, Neighborhood Restaurant Group, founded in 2010—and for which he serves as chairman of the board—that is focused on creating an equitable and sustainable local food system in the Washington area.

"We hear from parents and schools that a day out here has a big impact," he says, surveying the farm, its tidy rows of vegetables vibrantly green in the summer sun. "The kids go back and their interest in food is really elevated. They want to go grocery shopping with their parents, and they want to pick things out. They ask tough questions, and they're more adventurous eaters for being out here."

Encouraging positive connections with food is at the core of Michael's livelihood. "I grew up around food and people who cared about food and loved it," he says, of his upbringing in Baton Rouge, Louisiana. After an initial career on Capitol Hill, he decided to try his hand at running a business, and a restaurant felt like a logical choice. In 1997, he opened Evening Star Café in the Del Ray neighborhood of Alexandria—the first of what is now a portfolio of restaurants sixteen strong and growing, all guided by a commitment to quality ingredients grown as locally and sustainably as possible.

But something tugged at him: the desire to extend that focus on high-quality, sustainable food to the broader community he calls home. "As much as making a decision to go into the restaurant business, I made a decision to go into *business*," he explains. "Part of business ethics for me is, 'What is the impact? How can I make this meaningful in some way?'"

Arcadia Center for Sustainable Food & Agriculture is an effort to provide thoughtful answers to those questions by offering a multifaceted approach that includes the farm, mobile markets in several Washington-area neighborhoods, and a food hub that connects area farmers with the schools and individuals who need their produce the most.

"We're looking at the food system as a system, understanding if you set out to solve one problem in the system, you have inadvertent impacts on other parts," Michael explains. He cites the rise of farmers' markets as an example. "I think farmers' markets are wonderful and are a really important thing, but the typical farmers' market, right on the edge of a nice, affluent community, helped convince a lot of [less affluent] people, 'This food is not for us,'" he says. The answer, Michael hopes, lies in effecting change from a multitude of angles, as Arcadia hopes to do.

Even with all these efforts underway, Arcadia is just getting started, Michael says. The organization is working in partnership with the National Trust to expand Arcadia's presence at Woodlawn to encompass all of its 126 acres through a multifaceted, long-term plan that includes expanding the farming operation, adding a nursery for edible plants, a year-round farm stand, amphitheater, and a farmside restaurant to showcase the farm's bountiful harvest. It is an ambitious plan, and Michael is its ideal advocate.

"The idea of some kind of Arcadia-like commitment was always inherent in the way that I looked at how the business would work," he says. Across the farm, the campers are arriving, their excited voices filling the morning air. Michael grins.

"The question was really, 'How far do we have to go?'" he continues, eyes twinkling. "Turns out, we had to go pretty far." ●

> "Part of business ethics for me is, 'What is the impact? How can I make this meaningful in some way?'"

CHEESE

SPRING MILL FARM

CHEESEMAKER / **H.B. HUNTER** | REGION / **CAMPBELL COUNTY** | INFO / **SPRINGMILLFARM.NET**

Rooster calls echo across a farm in Campbell County as H.B. Hunter strides up to a large, fenced pasture where a couple of dozen goats stand serenely in the early morning light, watching him with casual interest. H.B. watches them back. Down the farm's worn dirt driveway, a voice calls, "Good morning!" as Jennifer Downey, the farm's owner, walks toward him, coffee mug in hand. She makes her way to where he is standing, and they watch the herd together. Jennifer has been raising goats for more than thirty years, making cheese and soap that she sold at farmers' markets in the Richmond and Lynchburg areas.

Thirteen miles up the road at Spring Mill Farm, on 80 acres of rolling Virginia farmland that has been in his family for generations, H.B. has been on his own cheesemaking journey. A farm loan officer at a local community bank, H.B.—short for Howlett Basil, a family name—holds a degree in dairy science, which included an internship at a farm creamery in Northern Virginia. He spent time out of the dairy world, but about five years ago, he decided to dedicate his evenings and weekends to cheesemaking, a pastime that quickly blossomed into a business as his goat's and cow's milk cheeses gained an enthusiastic following, taking hold first among restaurants and customers in the nearby Lynchburg area, and then spreading to points north and east.

He started leasing space and buying milk at a small creamery about 70 miles away, but as his business grew, it became clear he needed a facility closer to home that could accommodate the volume of cheese he was making. In just five years, Spring Mill Farm went from producing—and selling—20 pounds of cheese

"We have to learn to work together to be competitive, instead of trying to duplicate efforts on a really small scale, because it's so inefficient to do that."

per week to about 140 pounds, which included camembert, feta, a tomme-style raw goat's milk cheese, a crottin-style goat's milk cheese, and both plain and flavored chevre.

H.B. knew that to create a facility to the specifications and standards he desired, he would need to build it himself. He began constructing a creamery at his home on Spring Mill Farm and included a 50-gallon pasteurizer that could more than triple his processing capability. It is a pristine, carefully organized facility, and H.B. is incredibly proud. "We did every bit of it ourselves," he says, noting that his father helped with the construction each step of the way.

As the new Spring Mill Farm creamery debuted in the spring of 2015, H.B. faced another dilemma: he needed more milk. While he had a few goats, he knew that expanding the herd and managing it himself would stretch him too thin. One solution to

the problem seemed obvious and was right up the road: Jennifer's farm. He called her up, asking if he could start buying milk from her. She told him no.

Instead, she offered to come work for him.

At first, H.B. was dumbfounded. He'd known Jennifer as a fellow cheesemaker—in a state with only about forty—and as a competitor as well. A partnership on this level wasn't even on his radar, but it was something Jennifer had been considering for a while. She was feeling exhausted from the cycle of making small-batch cheeses and then driving long distances to sell them at market, all the while worrying about the farm and animals she was leaving behind.

"As much as I love the customers, and I have a following, it was too much for one person to do by themselves," she says. H.B.'s request for milk seemed like the perfect opportunity to pivot to what she loved most: managing a milking herd. So, she made the pitch to forgo cheesemaking and instead become his goatherd.

They agreed to mull it over and talk again in a few days. But it didn't take long before H.B. began to see the advantages of such a partnership. Jennifer's careful husbandry of her animals was well-respected, and many people across Virginia sought goats born at her farm for their strong bloodlines. Jennifer's offer would put these talents, and the wealth of knowledge that came with them, to work for H.B.'s cheesemaking business. Suddenly, it all made sense.

"I can focus on making cheese, which is what my passion is," H.B. says. "I love the animals and I love that part of it, but my real passion is making cheese. And hers is goats."

Under their arrangement, H.B. and Jennifer combined their respective goat herds, which live at Jennifer's farm. H.B. owns the herd and Jennifer handles the day-to-day management—ensuring the goats are milked, fed and cared for, and overseeing the breeding and kidding cycles as well, just as she has done for years. By isolating their strengths and combining efforts, H.B. feels he and Jennifer are piloting the kind of partnership that will be critical to the success of small farmers and producers in the coming decades. "This is where I see a lot of the future of small farming going," he says. "We have to learn to work together to be competitive, instead of trying to duplicate efforts on a really small scale, because it's so inefficient to do that."

"I look at the cheese business in Virginia as where the wine industry was fifteen years ago," he continues. "They were all working independently at that point and have all come together and seen what collaborative efforts can do for an industry."

H.B. and Jennifer now do something that neither could have foreseen even a year ago: work collaboratively to monetize H.B.'s herd of goats. Breeding season in the fall will give way to kidding in the late winter, providing the milk H.B. needs to help Spring Mill Farm grow. "I can sell all the cheese we can make right now," he says matter-of-factly, adding that he hopes to bump production up to 250 pounds per week in the next year to meet demand coming from Lynchburg, Charlottesville, and beyond. With his cheese gaining recognition from chefs and cheesemongers in an ever-widening area, Spring Mill Farm is rising to the top of the Virginia cheesemaking industry—with a little help.

"We have a different kind of arrangement than other places," Jennifer says. "These are his goats. I'm just the muscle."

"And the knowledge," H.B. quickly adds.

"This makes it a real, true partnership," Jennifer says.

H.B. nods. "It just works better for all of us." •

CHEESE CRAFTED BY GAIL HOBBS-PAGE AT CAROMONT FARM IN ESMONT, VIRGINIA

DANY SCHUTTE

CAREER / CHEESEMONGER + CORPORATE CHEESE BUYER
SOUTHERN SEASON / SOUTHERNSEASON.COM

Virginia's varied topography includes three distinct and remarkable swaths: the mountains, the Piedmont, and the seashore. And according to cheesemonger Dany Schutte, you can taste these distinct regions in the Commonwealth's cheese.

"We've got everything in Virginia except desert," says Dany, the corporate cheese buyer for specialty food retailer Southern Season. She explains that with artisanal cheese relying on animals that graze on Virginia grasslands, the soil's composition plays a pivotal role in the quality and flavor of the cheese. "We have a heavy clay soil through our Piedmont, which gets more mineral-rich as we move into the mountains. We have the effect of the sea table in the water along the coastline, as well as the sea breezes. All of that impacts the cheese development that's coming from each area," adds Dany, who also leads classes on topics such as pairing cheese with wine and craft beer as well as with dessert.

As with many other artisanal foods in Virginia, interest in producing artisan-crafted cheese is high, yet the barriers to entry are even higher as cheesemaking in the state evolves from a cottage industry into one with increased regulation—and refinement. "It used to be that a young cheesemaker could make cheese at home and sell it at a local farmers' market," Dany says. "We're gone from those days. You need to be in a proper facility."

Dany sees examples across Virginia of both established and nascent cheesemakers proving that they are up to the challenge of crafting artisanal cheese in the modern era. "We have great potential here," she says. "I hope to see some of these medium-level cheesemakers rise up to the occasion, tighten their facilities, and improve their craft."

CHEESEMONGER'S VA CHOICE

CURATED BY
NADJEEB CHOUAF
CHEESEMONGER
FLORA ARTISANAL CHEESE

TIMBERCREEK MARKET
CHARLOTTESVILLE, VIRGINIA

Meadow
Creek Dairy
Mountaineer
Galax, Virginia

Meadow Creek Dairy
Grayson
Galax, Virginia

The Virginia Chutney Co.
Spicy Plum Chutney
Washington, Virginia

"With the possibility of yearlong grazing and a community that actively seeks and supports local products, Virginia has always had the potential to be a great cheese-producing state. Thanks to established dairies like Meadow Creek and Caromont, as well as newcomers like Spring Mill Farm and Twenty Paces, we are really starting to see it happen."

Meadow
Creek Dairy
Appalachian
Galax, Virginia

Twenty Paces
Ricotta
Charlottesville, Virginia

CHEESE
Sourwood Farm
Wildflower Honey
Earlysville, Virginia

Jam According to Daniel
Fig Jam
Charlottesville, Virginia

Caromont Farm
Farmstead Chevre
Esmont, Virginia

CUTTING BOARDS
BLANC CREATIVES
CHARLOTTESVILLE, VIRGINIA

CHEESE KNIVES
MONOLITH STUDIO
IVY, VIRGINIA

RECIPE / **JASON ALLEY** | RESTAURANT / **PASTURE** | LOCATION / **RICHMOND** | INFO / **PASTUREVA.COM**

SPICY CAROMONT FARM PIMENTO GOAT CHEESE WITH SPICED HONEY

Caromont Farm, located in Albemarle County, began making its signature chevre in 2007.

Note from the Chef: I serve this spicy cheese spread with crusty bread, celery sticks, or my favorite, Ritz Crackers. It gets its heat from sambal, an Indonesian chili-based condiment that comes in many varieties, most commonly sambal oelek, which is available in Asian markets and many supermarkets. The cheese will keep for up to one week in the refrigerator.

FOR THE CHEESE:

12 oz. Caromont Farm Farmstead Chevre

1 small red bell pepper, roasted, peeled, and diced

2 Tbsp. sambal (see note)

1 Tbsp. chopped fresh tarragon

1 Tbsp. sliced green onion tops

½ cup Duke's mayonnaise

½ cup heavy whipping cream

Salt and pepper to taste

FOR THE HONEY:

1 tsp. yellow mustard seed

1 tsp. fennel seed

1 tsp. caraway seed

1 cup local honey

To make the cheese: Combine all the cheese ingredients in the bowl of a stand mixer. Starting on the lowest setting, whip the mixture, gradually increasing speed until the cheese is smooth and creamy.

To make the spiced honey: Toast the mustard, fennel, and caraway seeds in a sauté pan over medium-high heat until fragrant. Remove the pan from the heat, add the honey, and transfer it to a small bowl. Keep the honey warm until ready to serve.

To serve: Place a generous scoop of the cheese in the center of a plate, drizzle well with the honey, and serve with the accompaniment of your choice.

Jason Alley
Chef + Owner
Pasture

TASTEMAKER | DAVE MCINTYRE

WINE COLUMNIST / **THE WASHINGTON POST** | CAREER / **WRITER + COFOUNDER, DRINK LOCAL WINE** | INFO / **DMWINELINE.COM**

Dave McIntyre got into wine the way many people do: by visiting a winery. It was 1988, and Dave and his wife, Lily, were visiting friends in Alameda, California.

"We had done Yosemite, we had done San Francisco, and we had one day left," Dave recalls. "They said, 'What would you like to do?' and Lily and I said, 'How about Napa?'" Armed with recommendations of a few vineyards, they set off. By the third winery, they were sold, but it wasn't just the quality of the wine that impressed them.

"It was also seeing where it was made," Dave says, "and getting a little lesson in how it was made."

When they returned to their home outside Washington, D.C., Dave and Lily began looking for a similar experience closer to home. "We started visiting wineries around here," Dave says. "Through that, we watched the local wine industry grow and expand."

This burgeoning appreciation for wine from vine to glass captivated Dave's imagination, and he began to write about it. Twenty years later, he is the wine columnist for *The Washington Post* and a freelance wine writer with his own blog, WineLine—platforms he has used to share his appreciation of Virginia wine with a wide and growing audience. From the first days of his *Post* column, he hoped to broaden the wine conversation to include new areas of the country—an effort his editors embraced.

"They liked it a lot, and they supported it," he says.

Over the past two decades, Dave has watched the Virginia wine industry mature, supported by enthusiasts who fell in love with Virginia wine the same way he did, by discovering wine country in their own backyard.

"When you go to a winery, you meet people," Dave says. "You may meet the director or the winemaker behind the bar, pouring the wines. That's one of the nice things about having wine country here. Twenty years ago, when you said, 'I'm going to wine country,' you meant, 'I'm going to Napa,' or at least, 'I'm going to California.' Now you say, 'I'm going to wine country,' and you could mean Loudoun, Middleburg, Fauquier, Charlottesville. It's great."

With Virginia wines gaining traction with critics in mainstream wine publications, Dave feels the Commonwealth's winemakers have established their ability to produce world-class wines. The new goal, he says, is to expand the reach to people who haven't yet had the opportunity to experience and fall in love with Virginia wine country. To do that, quality must be the focus.

"The vintners are understanding the vineyards a little better; they're understanding the weather here and how to compensate for the rain and humidity," Dave says. "And they're learning how to get the grapes to ripen evenly to make better-quality wines." He is especially fond of the state's white wines, which he feels are top-notch.

Looking ahead, Dave sees opportunity for Virginia vineyards to enhance quality and production by carefully choosing the ideal sites for grape cultivation, which may include expanding into places such as the Shenandoah Valley. He also sees a new generation becoming interested in wine, which can further extend Virginia's reach.

"I think for wine lovers, and especially younger wine lovers, it's kind of cool to have wine country nearby," he says. "When you travel or visit friends, you can take them a bottle and say, 'Here's something you've never had before—and you're going to love it.'" •

> Twenty years ago, when you said, 'I'm going to wine country,' you meant, 'I'm going to Napa,' or at least, 'I'm going to California.' Now you say, 'I'm going to wine country,' and you could mean Loudoun, Middleburg, Fauquier, Charlottesville. It's great."

EARLY MOUNTAIN VINEYARDS

WINEMAKER / **BEN JORDAN** | REGION / **MADISON COUNTY** | INFO / **EARLYMOUNTAIN.COM**

t is the middle of August, and work is about to get very busy for Ben Jordan. His workday begins at 7 o'clock in the morning right now, but in the coming weeks, it will start as early as 4 a.m. Ben is the winemaker at Early Mountain Vineyards in Madison and for him, and hundreds of winemakers across Virginia, late summer is the harbinger of harvest.

Ben and his vineyard management team are out in the vines every day this time of year, monitoring the fruits' flavor, ripeness, sugar levels, and condition. They look for any damage from insects and animals, which are equally drawn to the ripening grapes. And while the team watches the vines, they also watch the forecast. Rain too close to harvest can dilute the fruits' sugar.

"You're racing time; you're racing nature. If you like the race, then it's fun," Ben says. "After a full growing season of watching vines, working with vines and growing fruit, then all of the sudden, you're turning fruit into wine."

It is a transformative time of year, and this Friday morning, Ben and Vineyard Manager Maya Hood White and Assistant Vineyard Manager Dustin Wade walk through the hillsides of vines in the early morning sun, checking on the Pinot Gris, Muscat Blanc and younger Chardonnay vines—the first varietals they will pick. From here, Ben can see a swath of Early Mountain's vineyard, its tidy rows flowing like ribbons across the hillsides. The tasting room rests in the valley below, and to the west Ben can see the familiar rise of the Blue Ridge Mountains. He grew up across those mountains, in the Shenandoah Valley, and his return to his native Virginia three years ago from California wine country was inspired by the opportunity to apply his love of winegrowing in his home state.

Surrounding him here in Madison County is that aspiration come to fruition: hands-on management of an estate vineyard, which is one facet of Ben's new role at Early Mountain that he relishes. He is also invigorated by Early Mountain's approach to growing its fruit, which for several years has focused on practices that seek to strengthen the vines from within, allowing Ben and his team to use a softer touch in the vineyard.

"What most wine lovers want from a wine is that it expresses a place and that it is true to what the vineyard gives."

"The more we can do in the vineyards, the less we have to do in the winery," Ben says, an earnest enthusiasm surfacing in his voice. "If the fruit is really good, then what you're trying to do is just express that, as opposed to a lot of technical tricks." Ben emphasizes the importance of organization, preparation, and diligence, but says nothing takes the place of growing the grapes properly, right from the start.

"What most wine lovers want from a wine is that it expresses a place and that it is true to what the vineyard gives," he says. "The more winemaking tricks you throw at it, the less transparent that is."

This idea of wine expressing a place—captured by the French term *terroir*—is central to Ben's focus as a winemaker, and understanding the varied terroir of Virginia is something he developed in his previous role as winemaker and general manager at Michael Shaps Wineworks in Charlottesville, which produces its own wines as well as those commissioned by its clients, using high-quality fruit sourced from throughout the Commonwealth. In his work there, Ben saw a vast array of vineyard types and locations and developed a sense for what combinations produce the finest fruit.

"I got to meet and talk to a lot of different people about what they're doing in their vineyard, versus what other people are do-

ing, and understand which vineyards work the best and why," Ben says. "It was invaluable."

It's a bird's-eye view of Virginia that will prove invaluable to Early Mountain, too, as it looks to Ben to further its focus on crafting first-rate wines, while also carefully increasing its production through adding more high-quality acres under cultivation. The importance of vineyard placement is one of the lessons Ben took away from his time at Wineworks.

"It's taken a while for the industry to figure out what produces the best vineyard sites," Ben explains. "The more that wineries do that and growers do that—the more they really search for the right site—the better that's going to be for Virginia."

Dovetailing with a better understanding of optimal vineyard placement is a clearer picture of the ideal management techniques for those vineyards—approaches tailored to Virginia's unique set of challenges.

"A lot of the techniques—and even winemaking products and vineyard products—that people use are based on other regions, and Virginia is its own thing," Ben explains.

This is where the Winemakers' Research Exchange comes into play. Launched by the Monticello Wine Trail in 2014, the group encourages participating winemakers to try controlled tri-

als on techniques in the field and in the cellar, with the aim of discovering winegrowing and winemaking approaches attuned to the particular needs of Virginia's climate and soil. A member of the collaborative group, Ben is hopeful that over time such efforts will further enhance the quality of wines crafted in his home state, now the fifth-largest producer of wine in the nation.

"That is the technical approach of this research group: to really figure out what is right for Virginia," he says, his enthusiasm evident. "Obviously, we're not going to figure it out in two years or ten years," he says, "but it's a gradual increase in understanding."

Ben sees the wine industry in Virginia at a critical moment, where it will begin to truly distinguish itself. Efforts such as the Winemakers' Research Exchange, combined with a better understanding of optimal vineyard placement and growing techniques, are all pieces of the Virginia viticulture puzzle that hundreds of vineyard owners and winemakers across the state have been piecing together for two decades. To advance its burgeoning wine industry, Ben believes that Virginia must inspire its next generation of winegrowers to learn how to grow grapes not in California or France, but right here in the Commonwealth.

"There are more and more instances of industry leaders whose approach to quality is inspiring the next generation, which will continue our growth," Ben says. "I am continually inspired by people like Jim Law of Linden Vineyards, Jeff White of Glen Manor Vineyards, and many of my peers." He notes that Jim has trained several winegrowers who have gone on to start their own vineyards in the state. Ben calls this a "momentum of inspiration"—one he feels shows that Virginia wine is growing the right way, from the ground up.

"A healthy industry has those sorts of grass roots," he says, his gaze resting on the vineyard in the valley below, where grapes are ripening in the Southern sun. "It's good for those of us who want to be in it for the long haul."

For Ben, and perhaps the entire Virginia wine industry, that long haul has only just begun. •

GABRIELE RAUSSE

CAREER / WINEMAKER + VINEYARD CONSULTANT
DIRECTOR OF GARDENS & GROUNDS, MONTICELLO
INFO / GABRIELERAUSSEWINERY.COM

Gabriele Rausse has deep roots in Virginia viticulture. In 1976, he helped establish award-winning Barboursville Vineyards—the start of a career that has now spanned 40 years and 47 Virginia vineyards. In that time, he has watched the state's wine industry transform from an afterthought into a showpiece of innovation and quality.

In Gabriele's mind, one of the strengths underpinning Virginia's wine industry is its openness to embracing new methods. Rather than relying on tradition to dictate choices in varietals and techniques, he sees Virginia vintners forging their own path—one that balances craft with science.

"Everything is based on the new knowledge of winemaking, and I think that is a wonderful thing," he says. "I am very happy with what has happened because there are a lot of wineries going in the right direction, in the sense that they want to make quality," he says. "There are so many people who do it because they fell in love with it."

The true test, Gabriele says, will be when Virginia vintners can sell their wines to the French and Italians. "We're not there yet, but we're going in that direction," he adds, voice brimming with confidence. "People will discover Virginia wine."

12 VA GEMS

CURATED BY
EARLY MOUNTAIN VINEYARDS
MADISON, VIRGINIA

Ankida Ridge Vineyards
Pinot Noir
Amherst County, Virginia
Nathan Vrooman—Winemaker

Blenheim Vineyards
Painted White
Albemarle County, Virginia
Kirsty Harmon—Winemaker

Boxwood Estate Winery
Topiary
Loudoun County, Virginia
Rachel Martin—Winegrower

Early Mountain Vineyards
Block Eleven
Madison County, Virginia
Ben Jordan—Winemaker

Glen Manor Vineyards
Sauvignon Blanc
Warren County, Virginia
Jeff White—Winemaker

King Family Vineyards
Petit Verdot
Albemarle County, Virginia
Matthieu Finot—Winemaker

Ox-Eye Vineyards
Scale House Reserve
Augusta County, Virginia
John Kiers—Winemaker

Pollak Vineyards
Meritage
Albemarle County, Virginia
Benoit Pineau—Winemaker

RdV Vineyards
Rendezvous
Fauquier County, Virginia
Rutger de Vink—Winegrower

Stinson Vineyards
Imperialis
Albemarle County, Virginia
Rachel Stinson Vrooman—Winemaker

Sunset Hills Vineyard
Mosaic
Loudoun County, Virginia
Nate Walsh—Winemaker

Veritas Vineyard & Winery
Viognier
Nelson County, Virginia
Emily Pelton—Winemaker

WINERIES LISTED IN
ALPHABETICAL ORDER

Fried Oysters with Celery Root Slaw and Rémoulade +
Afton Mountain Vineyards
Bollicine

Oysters with Champagne-Vinegar Mignonette +
Thibaut-Janisson Winery
Blanc de Chardonnay

Baked Oysters with Creamed Kale and Surryano Ham +
Chatham Vineyards
Church Creek
Steel-Fermented
Chardonnay

RECIPES + PAIRINGS | ROCKSALT

RECIPES / **DYLAN ALLWOOD** | RESTAURANT / **ROCKSALT** | LOCATION / **CHARLOTTESVILLE** | INFO / **ROCKSALTRESTAURANTS.COM**

OYSTERS WITH CHAMPAGNE-VINEGAR MIGNONETTE

At ROCKSALT in Charlottesville, Chef de Cuisine Dylan Allwood serves up raw oysters on the half shell with this classic mignonette—made piquant with a hand-crafted Champagne vinegar—along with a zesty cocktail sauce. Leftover mignonette will keep in the refrigerator for a week.

Makes enough sauce for 48 oysters.

- 1 cup Champagne vinegar
- 2 shallots, minced
- 2 tsp. freshly ground black pepper
- Crushed ice
- Freshly shucked Stingray Oysters from Rappahannock Oyster Co., or other large oysters
- Lemon wedges, for garnish

In a bowl, stir together vinegar, shallots, and pepper. Cover and chill.

To serve, fill a platter with crushed ice and arrange oysters on top, alongside small bowls of mignonette and cocktail sauce, with lemons for garnish.

Wine Pairing: Thibaut-Janisson Winery Blanc de Chardonnay Monticello AVA, Virginia

BAKED OYSTERS WITH CREAMED KALE AND SURRYANO HAM

Surryano ham is Virginia's answer to Serrano ham, made by the Edwards family in Surry, Va., using pork from free-range, humanely raised hogs that is dry-cured and hickory-smoked.

On a 250-acre dairy farm near Fairfield, Christie and Fred Huger make artisan cheeses from raw cow's milk, including their "McClure"

cheese specified here, though any semi-soft Swiss cheese will work.

Makes 12 servings.

- 4 ½ Tbsp. butter, divided
- 1 shallot, minced
- 2 cloves garlic, minced
- 3 Tbsp. flour
- ½ cup white wine
- 1 cup each: milk, heavy cream
- 2 oz. each: grated Swiss cheese (preferably Mountain View Farm's McClure), grated Parmesan
- Salt
- 2 bunches kale, stemmed, washed, and blanched
- 1 cup panko breadcrumbs
- 12 freshly shucked Rappahannock River Oysters from Rappahannock Oyster Co., or other large oysters
- 2 Tbsp. chopped Edwards Virginia Smokehouse Surryano ham, or other cured ham
- Coarse salt
- Lemon wedges, for garnish

In a saucepan, cook shallot and garlic in 2 ½ tablespoons butter until soft. Add flour, stir until smooth and cook for 2 to 3 minutes. Whisk in white wine, milk, and heavy cream and bring to a simmer. When thickened, whisk in cheeses and season with salt. Let mixture cool.

Squeeze water from blanched kale, chop coarsely and add to cheese sauce.

Melt remaining 2 tablespoons of butter in a small skillet, add breadcrumbs and cook over medium heat until toasted golden brown.

Preheat oven to 350 degrees. Put 1 tablespoon of cheese sauce on each oyster. Place on rimmed baking

sheet and bake for 7 to 8 minutes, or until oysters are hot and topping is golden brown. Sprinkle oysters with breadcrumbs and ham. Place oysters on a bed of coarse salt and garnish with lemons.

Wine Pairing: Chatham Vineyards Church Creek Steel-Fermented Chardonnay Northampton County, Virginia

FRIED OYSTERS WITH CELERY ROOT SLAW AND RÉMOULADE

Makes 10 servings, 6 oysters per person.

BREADING:

- 1 cup yellow cornmeal
- 2 cups flour
- Salt and freshly ground black pepper

CELERY ROOT SLAW:

- 1 small celery root, julienned
- ½ small red onion, julienned
- 2 stalks celery, sliced
- 1 Tbsp. each: chopped capers, chopped parsley, red wine vinegar
- 1 lemon, juiced
- 1 cup mayonnaise, preferably Duke's
- 2 tsp. sugar
- Salt and freshly ground black pepper

RÉMOULADE AND ASSEMBLY:

- 1 cup mayonnaise, preferably Duke's
- 1 tsp. each: red wine vinegar, Frank's RedHot sauce, lemon juice
- 1 Tbsp. each: Old Bay Seasoning, chopped parsley, minced pickle
- Vegetable oil, for frying

- 5 dozen freshly shucked Rappahannock River Oysters from Rappahannock Oyster Co., or other large oysters
- 3 Tbsp. minced chives, for garnish

In a bowl, add cornmeal, flour, and salt and pepper and stir well to combine.

In another bowl, combine celery root, onion, celery, capers, and parsley.

In a small bowl whisk together vinegar, lemon juice, mayonnaise, sugar, and salt and pepper to taste, then pour over vegetable mixture and toss to coat it.

Combine all the ingredients for the rémoulade in a small bowl.

Toss oysters in cornmeal mixture to coat. Working in batches, fry oysters in deep hot oil until golden brown and crisp. Drain on paper towels.

To serve, put a dollop of rémoulade on each plate and top with a portion of slaw. Place a fried oyster atop slaw, and garnish with chives.

Wine Pairing: Afton Mountain Vineyards Bollicine Nelson County, Virginia

Dylan Allwood
Chef de Cuisine
ROCKSALT

TASTEMAKER | JOSÉ ANDRÉS

CHEF + OWNER / **THINKFOODGROUP** | INFO / **THINKFOODGROUP.COM**

Sit down for a meal at America Eats Tavern in McLean, Virginia, and the menu you'll hold in your hands might feature dishes such as Mutton with Oysters, "Stewed" Cherry Tomatoes, and Vermicelli Prepared Like Pudding. These may sound as though they were invented for twenty-first-century palates, but each one is an early American recipe resurrected for the modern era. The mutton with oysters comes from *The New England Economical Housekeeper, and Family Receipt Book* from 1844, the stewed tomatoes originated from Charlottesville's historic Michie Tavern, while the vermicelli dish—the ancestor of today's macaroni and cheese—was created by Lewis Fresnaye, one of the country's first pasta makers, who included it with the coiled pasta he sold in Philadelphia in 1802.

Presenting these dishes for a contemporary audience is at the heart of America Eats Tavern because it feeds the soul of its founder, Chef José Andrés, who values the role of history in creating a sense of place. When José and his staff set out to create the restaurant's menu, they did their homework, tracing recipes back through the pages of history to bring them to the tables of today. One of the cookbooks that was central to the creation of America Eats Tavern was *The Virginia Housewife* by Mary Randolph. "It not only taught me about early American cooking, but also America's connections to the rest of the world," José says. The summertime menu at America Eats Tavern features gazpacho from an 1851 edition of that iconic cookbook.

"Virginia is the heart of American history," José observes. "It's where our Founding Fathers first started to harvest the land and from where the foundations for farming in this country grew."

The direct connection between land and food is fundamental to America Eats Tavern and all of José's restaurants—now twenty-one and counting, plus a food truck—which are concentrated in Washington, D.C., Virginia, and Maryland, and extend to California, Las Vegas, Miami, and Puerto Rico. At America Eats Tavern, the authenticity of the recipes finds its ideal expression in each dish's ingredients, which are heavily sourced from Virginia, Maryland, and the South.

"The right ingredients are all around us," José says, noting that his restaurants procure ingredients from producer-only farmers' markets throughout Washington, D.C., and the neighboring areas of Maryland and Northern Virginia. "That plays a huge role in how we are developing our menus," he explains. "Our menu at America Eats Tavern is entirely devoted to celebrating the bounty of Virginia by sharing its incredible flavors and ingredients with our guests."

> "Virginia is the heart of American history. It's where our Founding Fathers first started to harvest the land and from where the foundations for farming in this country grew."

The authentic American cuisine José and his team are crafting at America Eats Tavern extends beyond the plate to an entirely American wine list, a full quarter of which comes from the Commonwealth.

"I think the wine is very astonishing," José says. "Winegrowing in Virginia is not easy, and because of that, its winemakers have been making great advances in their art, from the site selection, to viticulture, to the actual making of the wine. So when you taste a Virginia wine, no matter what it is, you can be sure it was made with not only a lot of heart, but through a very deliberate process necessitated by the challenges they face."

The tireless work of the state's winegrowers, farmers, food artisans, and chefs represents the latest chapter in the story of Virginia—the place where American cuisine was born. It's a story José is telling through recipes and ingredients, and it's one that has captured his imagination.

"Every day," he says, "I keep discovering Virginia." ●

STEADFAST FARM

FARMER / **BRIAN WALDEN** | REGION / **ALBEMARLE COUNTY** | INFO / **STEADFASTFARM.ORG**

Like most farmers, Brian Walden spends a good bit of the current year thinking about what to plant in the next one. This year, he grew hard white wheat, hops, garlic, gingerroot, buckwheat, and hardy kiwi at Steadfast Farm, south of Charlottesville in Albemarle County. But next year might be different.

"Ten to twenty acres is the max you can do around here because of the terrain," he says, explaining the size of his cultivated fields, which he typically keeps to ten acres. "It's difficult terrain, but it's well-drained. There's great soil. There's plenty of moisture. It's just getting the varieties that do best here back here and established. That's what we've been doing year after year."

Year after year is now the better part of a decade. Brian has worked to resurrect the land—purchased by his parents in the 1980s—as a working farm, restoring it to its livelihood. In addition to a diverse array of crops, Steadfast's rolling pastures are home to thirty-five head of beef cattle. It's a lot of moving pieces, but he believes the time and effort are worthwhile.

"It's not as easy as it all sounds sometimes, but I've learned along the way," he says. "It's taken a long time. The learning curve doesn't end."

The crop mix at Steadfast today looks much different than it did even three years ago, when grains such as barley and wheat were more central to the farm's plan. Brian saw an opportunity to provide barley for the distilleries and breweries that were beginning to pop up all over Virginia. But he quickly found these plans complicated by two elements: weather and volume.

"Malting barleys have a hard time growing here on the East Coast because of the climate," Brian explains, adding that even if a farmer can cross the hurdle of growing barley in Virginia, many brewers and distillers require a significant, year-round volume

BRIAN WALDEN, HIS WIFE MIHR DANAË, AND THEIR CHILDREN

"It's not as easy as it all sounds sometimes, but I've learned along the way. It's taken a long time. The learning curve doesn't end."

of malted barley—volume they often seek in multiyear contracts with large providers, many of which are located in the western United States.

Wheat, too, has been a complicated venture. Virginia—whose high humidity increases the incidence of disease in the grain—has typically been an inhospitable place for cultivating high-quality hard wheats, the type required for bread flour. Six years ago, Brian started growing two varieties of hard winter wheats adapted for the East Coast—Appalachian White and NuEast, a red wheat. With these varieties, Brian envisioned a holistic approach to wheat farming.

"I thought I could be the grower, the miller, and the baker," he says, reflecting on that initial vision. It was a plan he found daunting to execute by himself. Luckily, not long into this journey, Brian learned about Woodson's Mill, a water-powered mill in Lowesville, Virginia, dating back to 1794, whose owner, Will Brockenbrough, was milling exclusively Virginia-grown grain.

"He was just getting started and called me up," Brian recalls. "I brought several hundred pounds down to him."

Those several hundred pounds of Virginia wheat were the first to be delivered to the mill in more than sixty years, and Will ground it into whole wheat flour using 1840s-era millstones. For Brian, the resulting product was the ideal expression of the hard-fought battle to grow hard wheats in the state.

"I saw it as a way to market the product in a consistent fashion," Brian says of his partnership with Will, a man he says clearly loves both Woodson's Mill and the craft of milling. "That's what you need," says Brian. "I saw that in him, and I wanted to be part of it."

Brian's partnership with Woodson's Mill has been crucial to increasing the product's marketability. But stone-ground whole wheat, though appealingly wholesome, is more of a challenge to use than all-purpose and pastry flours, which have had the coarse, fibrous germ and bran removed from the grain. So, in the fall of

2015, Woodson's is adding additional sifting screens that will allow it to start making these more refined flours—widening its reach, and in turn, that of Steadfast.

"If you can create more diverse flours, you have more diverse avenues to sell it," Brian explains.

As he looks ahead to what he will plant in the coming months and years, Brian returns to this idea of enhancing value. The types of crops he is growing at Steadfast, especially the grains and beans, need some form of processing to be optimally marketable. For beans, Brian hopes to see a processing facility open in the Charlottesville area, one that could make hummus, a product he has tested at farmers' markets, to rave reviews.

"There's very limited processing here for that value-adding component that is essential to extending the harvest, extending the paychecks, and getting the consumers, the distributors, the grocery stores to have a consistent product," he says.

After six years of growing wheat, Brian is considering crop rotation to replenish the soil and lessen the threat of disease. He will continue to grow beans and buckwheat—a summer crop he has just begun to cultivate for harvest, rather than its more traditional use as a cover crop. It was an experiment of sorts that he undertook at Will's request, and it led to the creation of a pancake mix of whole wheat flour, cornmeal, and buckwheat—a blend that is delightfully rich in flavor without being too heavy in texture. Both Brian and Will are thrilled with the result.

"Buckwheat flour is another example of a great local food source that is non-gluten, that makes a flour, that's super nutritious, that is available," Brian says. It is also a higher-dollar-per-bushel crop, so there is an incentive to grow buckwheat—as long as there is a demand for it.

Demand. In the end, that has been perhaps the longest learning curve Brian has faced since founding Steadfast Farm. For each of the crops he grows, he sees some local demand, but he feels that demand is at times tenuous and often lacks the infrastructure needed to increase it. The key, then, is helping to bolster interest more broadly and to keep educating consumers on the value of locally sourced foods. "It is hard," Brian says of the effort to grow these kinds of crops. "And that's the value."

Steadfast Farm has come a long way in the past decade, and Brian continues to steward it as he does the land that comprises it—with pragmatism, enthusiasm, and care.

"I wanted to get into the local food market and try to support it, because I knew I could," Brian says. "I want to see it succeed. I want to see more people get into it. I want to see success in every component of it." •

WOODSON'S MILL

OWNER + MILLER / **WILL BROCKENBROUGH**
INFO / **WOODSONSMILL.COM**

Woodson's Mill has been in existence since 1794, and Will Brockenbrough reckons that it has only stopped milling grain twice, for a total of about 30 years.

"There's not much else you can do with a building like this," he explains. "If you want to preserve it, you have to use it. The best way to make use of it is to make it earn its keep, and that's what it's doing."

Will is the latest steward of this water-powered mill in Lowesville, named for Julian Belmont Woodson, a medical doctor and Virginia state senator who owned it for the first half of the 20th century. Gill Brockenbrough, Will's father, purchased and restored the mill in the 1980s with the help of Steve Roberts, a

Nelson County native who has served as the head miller for 30 years. When his father died in 2001, Will became the new resident owner, and under his stewardship, Woodson's Mill has become dedicated to milling Virginia-grown grains—including corn, wheat, and buckwheat—using the same two millstones installed in an expansion to the mill in the 1840s. In just three years' time, Will has gone from milling 400 pounds of corn at a time to more than a ton, and he has customers across the Commonwealth.

"The local food movement has been critical to its success," Will says. "People actually care about this now, about where their grains come from, how they're milled, how they're cooked. Without that, we wouldn't be here. We wouldn't be able to do this."

Wheat

All-Natural
Whole Wheat Flour

Three-Grain Pancake Mix

Buckwheat

Corn

All-Natural Grits

GRAINS FROM VA

VIRGINIA-GROWN GRAINS MILLED AT
WOODSON'S MILL
LOWESVILLE, VIRGINIA

5-Grain Batard
MarieBette Bakery
and Café
Charlottesville, Virginia

Prepared
**Three-Grain
Pancakes**

Prepared
Grits

WOODSON'S MILL SOURCES
BUCKWHEAT FROM **STEADFAST FARM**
IN ALBEMARLE COUNTY, VIRGINIA,
AND CORN AND WHEAT FROM
SEVERAL FARMS THROUGHOUT
THE COMMONWEALTH.

HAND-FORGED SKILLET
PAN AND SPATULA BY
BLANC CREATIVES
CHARLOTTESVILLE, VIRGINIA

RECIPES + PAIRINGS | THE RED HEN

RECIPES / **MATT ADAMS & BECCA NORRIS** | RESTAURANT / **THE RED HEN** | LOCATION / **LEXINGTON** | INFO / **REDHENLEX.COM**

At The Red Hen in Lexington, Virginia, Chef Matt Adams and Chef Becca Norris create a new menu each day based on the freshest ingredients available from local farms and artisans. One of their partners in this farm-to-table focus is Wade's Mill, a family-owned, water-driven flour mill built around 1750 that uses millstones to grind its flours and grits.

The Red Hen sources eggs from local producers including Paradox Farm and Flying Fox Farm.

WADE'S MILL CORNBREAD

Note from the Chefs: We enjoy our cornbread fresh for dinner, but if you find you have some left over the next day, bake up a batch of our delicious cornbread pudding (recipe follows).

1 cup (142 g) Wade's Mill Yellow Cornmeal

3 ½ cups (425 g) all-purpose flour

4 ½ tsp. (18 g) sugar

4 tsp. (14 g) baking powder

1 tsp. (5 g) baking soda

1 tsp. (7 g) salt

1 ⅓ cups (326 g) buttermilk

1 ⅓ cups (326 g) whole milk

4 Paradox Farm eggs

1 stick (112 g) butter, melted

Adjust oven rack to middle position and heat oven to 425 degrees. Butter a 13 by 9-inch baking dish.

Whisk cornmeal, flour, sugar, baking powder, baking soda, and salt together in large bowl. In a separate bowl, whisk buttermilk, milk, eggs, and melted butter. Stir the milk mixture into the dry ingredients and mix until just combined.

Pour batter into prepared baking dish. Bake about 24 minutes, rotating pan about halfway through, until top is golden brown and a toothpick inserted into the center comes out clean.

RED HEN CORNBREAD PUDDING

Note from the Chef: I like to top this pudding with sweet cream ice cream from Sweet Things Ice Cream Shoppe in Lexington, Virginia, and some compote made with huckleberries from Digger Jays in Verona, Virginia (recipe follows). I prefer to bake the pudding in small, nonstick silicone molds, but feel free to use any oven-proof baking dish. Just keep in mind that cooking times may change.

2 to 2 ½ qt. leftover cornbread, diced into 1-inch cubes

CUSTARD BASE:

2 ¼ cups (567 g) heavy cream

½ cup (113 g) sugar

1 Flying Fox Farm duck egg

5 Flying Fox Farm duck egg yolks

½ Tbsp. (12 g) vanilla extract

2 tsp. (6 g) ground cinnamon

Adjust oven rack to middle position and heat oven to 350 degrees. Butter several small silicone molds.

Put all the ingredients for the custard base into a blender and blend until smooth. Place cornbread in a large bowl and pour over it just enough of the custard base to completely saturate it. Lightly fluff the cornbread-custard mixture with your hands. Try not to break it up too much.

Place a generous helping of the creamy bread mixture into the molds, filling them nearly to the top.

Place molds in a large roasting pan. Pour enough hot tap water into the pan to reach about three-quarters of the way up the sides of the molds.

Carefully set the pan in the oven and bake for about 1 hour, or until puffed and golden and the center registers 160 to 175 degrees on an instant-read thermometer.

Remove from oven and let rest until molds are cool enough to remove from the water. Serve with ice cream and huckleberry compote, if desired.

HUCKLEBERRY COMPOTE

Note from the Chef: This compote makes a good topping for bread pudding and other desserts. Leftover compote is also delicious on a stack of pancakes.

2 Tbsp. granulated sugar

1 pint huckleberries

¼ cup water

Dash salt

Add sugar to a heavy-bottomed pan and place over medium heat. The sugar will melt and then start to brown as it caramelizes. When it turns a light amber color, carefully add the berries all at once and then stir in the water. The caramelized sugar will seize up at first and then begin to dissolve again.

When the sugar is completely dissolved, strain the liquid from the berries and set them aside. Pour the juice back into the pan and reduce it over medium heat until it thickens. Add salt and then pour the reduction over the berries. Stir to combine, and let cool.

Matt Adams + Becca Norris Chefs The Red Hen

TASTEMAKER | TARVER KING

CHEF / **THE RESTAURANT AT PATOWMACK FARM** | INFO / **PATOWMACKFARM.COM**

"You ever had a miracle berry?" Tarver King asks. He strides across the kitchen garden at The Restaurant at Patowmack Farm in the direction of a shrub with oblong, pointed green leaves and small clusters of bright-red berries. He plucks a few. "It almost tastes like a bland cranberry," he explains. "When you chew it, let the juices stay on your palate for a minute, and then go ahead and swallow it. It takes a minute or two to take effect." He then heads for the kitchen for step two of the demonstration.

Synsepalum dulcificum is the name of this plant. A native of West Africa, the berries contain a protein—miraculin—that binds to the tongue's taste buds. "What the miracle berry does is stops you from being able to perceive anything but sweetness," Tarver explains, doling out slices of fresh lime. "This is just a straight-up lime," he continues, "but it's going to taste like limeade."

"We're able to show what a really good food experience can be using everything from right here."

He's right—the sourness of the lime vanishes completely, leaving only a sweet essence in its wake. It's astonishing, and that experience is part of what Tarver loves about his work as the executive chef at The Restaurant at Patowmack Farm in Lovettsville, Virginia. "We never would have been able to grow and experiment and try something like that anywhere else," he says.

Patowmack, a 40-acre farm overlooking the Potomac River, was founded by owner Beverly Morton Billand nearly thirty years ago. The farm was originally an organic garden, but the produce Beverly raised gained such a following that she eventually opened a restaurant on the property. Now, more than an acre of the farm is dedicated to the cultivation of organic vegetables, berries, and fruits that Tarver and his staff use at the restaurant.

"We grow everything," he says, explaining that the farm even produces a host of different eggs from geese, ducks, chickens, and turkeys. The area's rich agricultural offerings allow Patowmack Farm to source anything it doesn't grow from local farmers, while its wooded, river bluff terrain provides Tarver and his team with foraged ingredients such as mushrooms and pawpaws, seed pods of a tree with the same name, native to the region, with a flavor and consistency similar to banana.

With this bounty, Tarver creates three seven-course menus each night: *Found*, featuring food that is foraged; *Grown*, centering on food from Patowmack Farm; and *Raised*, utilizing foods from humanely raised animals. The menus change constantly, depending on what is in season, or, in winter, what Tarver pulls out of the larder, which is stocked with fermented foods and preserves that he and his team put up throughout the growing season.

The restaurant has a dedicated following, with Saturday seatings booked months in advance. Yet despite this popularity, The Restaurant at Patowmack Farm is open for regular business only on Thursdays, Fridays, and Saturdays—a schedule Tarver believes allows for improved quality of life for the staff, increased focus and creativity in the menu, and a richer guest experience. Combined with the farm's on-site bounty, it's a holistic approach he hopes to see catch on.

"Patowmack has been so much more than I could have ever hoped for," he says. "We're able to show what a really good food experience can be using everything from right here." ●

THREE NOTCH'D BREWING COMPANY

HEAD BREWER / **MARY MORGAN** | CITY / **HARRISONBURG** | INFO / **THREENOTCHDBREWING.COM**

In the brewhouse at Three Notch'd Brewing Company on East Market Street in Harrisonburg, head brewer Mary Morgan prepares to measure the sugar level in one of her beers in progress to determine if it is ready to move to refrigeration. This is called taking the gravity of a beer. To do so, Mary uses an instrument called a hydrometer—a glass cylinder with an accompanying bulbed stem that measures the density of liquid. The higher the sugar content, the denser the liquid and the higher the hydrometer's bulb will float.

Today, Mary is testing a beer called "Uncle Cyrus" Dark American Wheat. She fills the glass cylinder with the brew, slips the hydrometer stem into the beer and crouches down to read the result. She stands up, nodding. "It's ready now to move into the cold condition," she says.

Mary truly savors the hands-on work of a craft beer brewmaster. "I like that I touch every part of the process," she says. "I do the kegging. I touch all the ingredients, and I'm mashing by hand. I don't just push buttons on my brew system. It makes me feel a lot more connected to the product."

She is also quick to admit that the science behind brewing is a major draw. Outside of her role as a brewmaster for Three Notch'd, she is a biology and chemistry teacher at a local high school as well as an avid gardener. Like many professional brewers, Mary started out as a homebrewer. When she heard that Three Notch'd—which launched in 2013 with a flagship brewhouse in Charlottesville— was looking for a part-time brewer for a new Harrisonburg location, she called brewmaster Dave Warwick and threw her hat in the ring. She was on-site for the first brew day, and it was immediately clear to Dave that he need look no further.

"She's ten times more creative than I am," says Dave, an award-winning brewmaster who says his strength lies in formulating approachable brews that keep more firmly to style, such as Hydraulion, an Irish-style red, and 40 Mile, an India pale ale. "I really thought it was essential to bring her in because she has a lot to offer with local ingredients. She has her own, in her own garden. It doesn't get any more local than that."

Dave provides the Harrisonburg brewery with the Three Notch'd flagship beers, as well as the seasonal brews. "That frees her up to let her creativity flow and brew whatever the heck she wants," he says.

Since the Harrisonburg brewhouse and taproom opened in May 2014, Mary has made a name for herself as a prolific brewmaster of small-batch beers, debuting a new brew each week. In the first year the brewery was open, she made 45 unique beers, creating her own recipes every time. "Inspiration can be drawn from a lot of different places," she says, including flavors in food and even people's personalities. In every beer, she tries to incorporate at least one locally sourced ingredient, including honey, pumpkins, hops and strawberry leaves—many of these from her large garden.

Of the beers she's created since becoming brewmaster at Three Notch'd Harrisonburg, the biggest gamble was the Sweet Potato Jamaican Curry, which used locally grown sweet potatoes. "I thought I was going to get shot down on that one," she says, chuckling. "But they let me go for it and it actually sold really well."

The secret to this success may be Harrisonburg itself. It's a town that values artistic creativity, says Betsy O'Brien, the brewery's tasting room manager. "The culture is very art-centric and quirky," she explains, qualities that are evident in the taproom, where everything from wall hangings to tasting flight boards are local-artist originals.

"Harrisonburg Three Notch'd is very different from Charlottesville Three Notch'd," Betsy says, "and I think it's a reflection of the town and what people want here," she says. "Harrisonburg is all about community, so the more something touches, the better it is."

This focus on collaboration is front and center in Mary's work in the brewhouse, not only in her use of locally grown ingredients but also in the distinctive brews she has created for local restaurants, bars and even musicians. "When I sit down for a collaboration, I tell whomever I'm meeting with that this is a

"There's not a bad meal to have in this town. There's great beer to drink in this town. It's got the perfect mix of everything I need."

blank slate," she explains. "Think about that flavor that you've wanted in your mouth when you've had a beer, but you haven't had it yet. Let's create something new." This has led to collaborations such as Blame Canada, a high-gravity, oaked amber beer produced for Capital Ale House; Miss Mary's Muffins, a blueberry muffin-inspired beer for local coffeehouse and bar The Artful Dodger; and Golden Pony, an American pale ale crafted for The Golden Pony restaurant —a beer so successful that Dave brewed it at the big brewhouse in Charlottesville and distributed it throughout Virginia.

When she talks about these collaborations, it is clear that Mary deeply loves where she lives. "There's not a bad meal to have in this town," she observes, earnestly. "There's great beer to drink in this town. It's got the perfect mix of everything I need."

For Dave, who has now seen two Three Notch'd brewhouses rise to success in two very different communities, passing the litmus test of Harrisonburg is a real accomplishment and makes him hopeful about the brand's ability to continue to expand amid Virginia's thriving, though nascent, craft beer industry, which is roughly 120 breweries strong—growth Dave attributes to both a national trend toward craft beverages and Virginians' refined palate, which he credits to the state's thriving wine industry.

"I never dreamed two years ago that we would be here—literally here," he says. "The true test was how the brand was accepted in Harrisonburg, and it's doing really well."

Noting that the Three Notch'd motto "Leave Your Mark" pays homage to Virginians who have affected the course of American history, Dave feels that—thanks in large part to Mary's beermaking prowess—Three Notch'd has found a permanent home in Harrisonburg, evolving its brand while keeping its identity.

"We have stayed true to what we wanted from the beginning," he says. "We're trying to leave our humble little mark in the craft beer world."

And in the midst of Three Notch'd expanding, of leaving that humble mark, this city in the Shenandoah Valley has left its mark on them, too. •

CHARLOTTESVILLE HOPS LLC

OWNERS + FOUNDERS / CHRIS GORDON + GORDON GIULIANO
INFO / CHARLOTTESVILLEHOPS.COM

A handful of cars and pickup trucks bounce along a cow pasture in Ivy, Virginia, early on a summer morning, all headed to the same destination: a third-acre hop yard, where long ropes host lush vines bedecked in brilliant green cones of Cascade hops. It's harvest day at Charlottesville Hops in Ivy, where Chris Gordon and Gordon Giuliano put out the call to friends and neighbors to pull up a chair and help with the harvest, plucking the fragrant cones off the long vines, one by one.

Hop farming is on the rise in Virginia amid an explosion of craft breweries, many of which are looking to reflect their communities in the beers they brew. Whether it's local hops, honey or barley, this taste of place is one of the elements putting craft beer in the state at the top of its field.

Chris and Gordon will send all the hops harvested here—81 pounds by day's end—to Three Notch'd Brewing Company in nearby Charlottesville, where Brewmaster Dave Warwick will combine them with those grown by other Virginia hop farmers in a beer called 10* Farmers IPA—one of Dave's favorite seasonal brews. "It's a great way of paying homage and giving a spotlight to the local hop farmers of Virginia," he says.

BEER RUN'S VA PICKS

CURATED BY
BEER RUN
CHARLOTTESVILLE, VIRGINIA

AleWerks Brewing Company
Washington's Porter
Williamsburg, Virginia

Blue Mountain Brewery
Dark Hollow—Bourbon Barrel-Aged
Imperial Stout
Afton, Virginia

Brothers Craft Brewing
Hoptimization—India Pale Ale
Harrisonburg, Virginia

Champion Brewing Company
Tart—Berliner-Style Weisse
Charlottesville, Virginia

Chaos Mountain Brewing
Agents Of Chaos Belgian
Special Dark
Callaway, Virginia

Devils Backbone Brewing Company
Eight Point IPA
Roseland, Virginia

Hardywood Park Craft Brewery
Hardywood Singel—Belgian Abbey-
Style Blonde Ale
Richmond, Virginia

Lickinghole Creek Craft Brewery
Bourbon Barrel Three Chopt Tripel
Goochland, Virginia

Parkway Brewing Co.
Raven's Roost Baltic Porter
Salem, Virginia

Port City Brewing Company
Optimal Wit Belgian-Style White Ale
Alexandria, Virginia

Starr Hill Brewery
Grateful Pale Ale
Crozet, Virginia

Three Notch'd Brewing Company
40 Mile IPA
Charlottesville, Virginia

BREWERIES LISTED IN
ALPHABETICAL ORDER

Killer Kolsch
Champion Brewing
Company

**Factory Girl
Session IPA**
Parkway Brewing
Company

MEXICAN STREET CORN

Chef Ian Boden gives a Southern spin to the classic Mexican street food of grilled corn slathered with a creamy, chili-spiked sauce—known as elote, a Nahuatl word for corn on the cob—adding peanuts from Virginia and soy sauce from Kentucky.

Note from the Chef: It is important to use a hot sauce with no emulsifiers, such as Tabasco or Crystal. Store leftover peanuts in the refrigerator, where they will keep for several months. Leftover sauce will keep for a week refrigerated.

4 ears sweet corn, shucked

FOR THE PEANUTS:

1 cup raw Virginia peanuts, shelled and skinned

½ cup soy sauce, preferably Bourbon Barrel Foods' Bluegrass Soy Sauce

¼ cup apple cider vinegar

¼ cup rice wine vinegar

1 medium-size knob of fresh ginger, smashed

1 jalapeño pepper, halved

1 cup water

2 Tbsp. sugar

FOR THE HOT-SAUCE MAYONNAISE:

1 whole egg

1 egg yolk

Juice from 1 lime

Salt to taste

2 cups grapeseed or other neutral-flavored oil

½ cup hot sauce (see note)

Cilantro sprigs, for garnish

To prepare the corn: On a hot grill or griddle pan, slowly roast the corn until it is bright yellow, with nice dark charred spots all the way around.

To prepare the peanuts: Put all the ingredients for the peanuts in a saucepan and bring to a slow simmer. Cook, stirring occasionally, until peanuts are tender but still keep their shape, about 45 minutes. Discard ginger and pepper halves.

For the hot-sauce mayonnaise: While the peanuts are simmering, in a small pan, bring hot sauce to a boil and reduce to about one-third cup. In a bowl, whisk the egg, egg yolk, lime juice, and a pinch of salt. Slowly drizzle the oil into the egg mixture, a few drops at a time, whisking constantly. Once you have a strong emulsion, you may increase the flow of oil. Keep whisking until all the oil is incorporated. Stir in the hot sauce and taste for seasoning, adding salt if needed.

To serve: Spread the hot-sauce mayo all over the corn, then sprinkle the pickled peanuts on top along with sprigs of cilantro.

Paired with: Killer Kolsch
Champion Brewing Company
Charlottesville, Virginia

WATERMELON-CUCUMBER SALAD WITH SURRYANO HAM AND PICKLED PEPPERS

Chef Ian Boden likes to incorporate Virginia ingredients in this refreshing salad—ham from Edwards Virginia Smokehouse and goat's milk feta from Caromont Farm. He also uses other artisanal ingredients crafted in the South for this dish: oil from Georgia Olive Farms in Georgia and salt from J.Q. Dickinson Salt-Works in West Virginia. He recommends making the pickled peppers at least two days in advance, but they will still be delicious if eaten immediately.

1 cup hot banana peppers, sliced into rings

FOR THE PICKLING BRINE:

⅓ cup white vinegar

⅔ cup water

1 tsp. kosher salt

2 tsp. sugar

1 garlic clove, peeled and left whole

½ tsp. black peppercorns

½ tsp. coriander seeds

½ tsp. yellow mustard seeds

FOR ASSEMBLING:

1 pound seedless watermelon, cut into large dice

1 large cucumber, peeled, seeded, and cut into ½-inch slices

Juice of 2 limes

¼ cup olive oil, plus more for drizzling

Ham, about 4 oz., thinly sliced or grated

¼ pound feta

Salt and pepper, to taste

Fresh mint, cilantro, parsley, or chives, for garnish (optional)

To prepare the pickling brine: Place all the ingredients for the brine in a small, nonreactive pot and bring to a simmer. Put the sliced peppers into a glass jar. Pour hot brine over peppers. Cover and let cool to room temperature.

To assemble the salad: In a mixing bowl, toss the watermelon and cucumbers with a good pinch of salt, freshly cracked pepper, the lime juice, and the ¼ cup of olive oil. Transfer to a serving bowl or tray and then arrange the ham, feta, and pickled peppers on top. Finish with a drizzle of olive oil, a couple of cranks of black pepper, and garnish with herbs, if desired.

Paired with: Factory Girl Session IPA
Parkway Brewing Company
Salem, Virginia

Ian Boden
Chef + Owner
The Shack

Walk down Main Street in Marshall, Virginia, and you can see a transformation is afoot. Old storefronts show signs of new life, punctuated by fresh paint and the hum of saws and pounding of hammers. A few blocks away, plans are in motion to add hundreds of modest homes, part of a five-year reimagining of this town of 1,500 in northwestern Fauquier County. Marshall is on the cusp of a very intentional change, and Neal and Star Wavra are central figures in that story.

"As soon as we walked in, we knew it would be perfect," says Star, recalling their first glimpse inside 8369 West Main Street, a rambling building featuring sections dating from the 1790s and mid-1800s, where every corner radiates history and heritage. A private residence for many decades, it was once a local restaurant, and that's the identity Neal and Star are looking to recapture in a complete renovation of the building into Field & Main Restaurant.

With a decade each in the hospitality industry, including five years as the innkeepers at the Ashby Inn in nearby Paris, Virginia, Star and Neal had been mulling opening their own restaurant for a long time, but they wanted to attune their concept to a space, rather than the other way around. "It wasn't like we were looking for a place to put our restaurant," Star says. "It was like we found the place, and now we're building around it."

"As you come in the door, you are going to be welcomed and embraced by a comfortable place," Neal explains, emphasizing that while not a casual eatery, Field & Main will have a relaxed atmosphere. "We've spent our whole lives in fine dining and love the experience of fine dining," he continues. "But communities don't gather at fine dining places. This was built for that—it's a gathering place."

As they work to shape each room of Field & Main into its new identity—including dining rooms and a hometown bar—Neal and Star are keeping the community of Marshall at the center of their vision. Down the street, The Whole Ox artisan butcher shop is setting up in a new location after outgrowing its original space in The Plains, and Warrenton-based Red Truck Bakery has added a new location across the way. Neal, who has dedicated his professional career to making the farm-to-table model viable, sees the transformation of Marshall's Main Street as an opportunity to take that idea to the next level.

"We can work together to buy product from farms," Neal explains, noting that instead of buying just a small amount of produce for his restaurant, cooperative buying with the butcher and bakery could allow all three businesses to truly support local

---

"It's not farm to one table—it's a farm to one *town*."

---

farms through buying in volume. "It's not farm to one table—it's a farm to one *town*," he says.

Neal and Star are dedicated to making Field & Main accessible to everyone in Marshall, including the producers supplying their ingredients. "All the roads in the olden days ran from a field to main street, or from main street out to a field," Neal says. "We want those products to be showcased here, and the people who make those products and the people who enjoy those products to have a place to go."

Here amid the sturdy, storied walls of Field & Main, it's impossible not to feel Neal and Star's palpable enthusiasm for the grassroots reinvention happening in Marshall, and in communities across Virginia. Neal notes that in the era of online retailers, main streets across America must find a new identity.

"We need a place to gather," he says. "I think Main Street's that kind of place." •

"The local food movement in Virginia has grown tremendously. The variety of crops and products on the market is much more diverse and consistent; producers are improving their packaging and quality; and there is a vibrant community of twentysomethings who are bringing new life and hipness to producing local food. Consumers are also more educated and thoughtful in purchasing food. They are going to far more of an effort to buy local, and they value small-batch and sustainable production methods."

— KATE COLLIER
CO-OWNER + COFOUNDER
FEAST!
INDEPENDENT SPECIALTY FOOD STORE
CHARLOTTESVILLE, VIRGINIA

FARM TABLE SPREAD BY **TRACEY LOVE** OF **HILL AND HOLLER**, FEATURING TABLEWARE FROM **ROXIE DAISY**, MEAT AND CHEESE FROM **TIMBERCREEK MARKET**, AND AN APPLE PIE FROM **THE PIE CHEST**—ALL BASED IN CHARLOTTESVILLE, VIRGINIA.

AFTERWORD

BY OUR LOCAL COMMONS

In the summer of 2015, we traveled across the Commonwealth of Virginia, collecting the stories featured in the pages of this book. Day after day, mile after mile, we were astounded and invigorated by the talent, passion, and generosity of the individuals and families who dedicate their lives and livelihoods to feeding their fellow Virginians.

We learned how water-powered millstones work, the mechanics of a dairy pipeline system, and the benefits of single-varietal apple pressing. We picked hops, tasted smoked cider, and fell deeply in love with homemade biscuits. We came to understand the importance of genetics in grass-fed beef herds and the complex timing of a vineyard harvest. We got lost in conversations about food sustainability, thoughtful menu development, and neighborhood revitalization. We gained a deeper appreciation of Virginia's pivotal role in American cuisine, became intrigued by the possibilities of culinary storytelling, and gained new insights into the challenges of adapting old-world viticulture to new-world soil.

This journey underscored for us, yet again, the incredible energy driving this food revolution in Virginia. For the past several years, Our Local Commons has immersed itself in the Commonwealth's local food communities, producing collections of richly told stories—including *Our Local Commons–Charlottesville* Vol. I and Vol. II—that illuminate the work of those building a new era in American food. This is a movement with deep roots and even deeper passions to build a better food system: one that harnesses the skill and knowledge of local producers to strengthen local economies and ensure that every single person has ready access to fresh, healthy food. A lofty goal, perhaps, but we have met Virginians with the skill and dedication to bring this vision to life—and they are doing so every day.

When we embarked upon creating *The Virginia Table* with our friends at Early Mountain Vineyards, we were excited by the opportunity to deepen our understanding of Virginia's foodways and share its stories with a broader audience. The journey that ensued was more intriguing, challenging, and satisfying than we ever could have imagined. It filled us with abiding respect for those who work tirelessly toward a shared dream for their families, their communities, and their common wealth—the land they call home.

Our work is but a reflection of theirs, and it is a privilege to share their stories with you here.

Warmly,
Jenny, Andrea + Sarah

Our Local Commons
ourlocalcommons.com

ACKNOWLEDGMENTS

The Virginia Table was produced through a collaborative partnership between Early Mountain Vineyards and Our Local Commons. We offer our gratitude to all the artisans who participated in this project, welcoming us into their homes and workplaces and sharing with us their stories, skills, and insights. Special thanks to the many vendors who lent their talents, products, and time, especially Tracey Love, Roxie Daisy, Timbercreek Market, Blanc Creatives, and Monolith Studios.

EARLY MOUNTAIN VINEYARDS

earlymountain.com

PROJECT MANAGER
Rachel Kennedy Caggiano, *Marketing Director*

CREATIVE CONSULTANT
Dave Kostelnik, *General Manager*

CREATIVE ADVISORS
Peter Hoehn
Erich Broksas
Jade Floyd

OUR LOCAL COMMONS

ourlocalcommons.com

CREATIVE DIRECTOR + PHOTOGRAPHER
Andrea Hubbell
andreahubbell.com

DIRECTOR OF PHOTOGRAPHY + PHOTOGRAPHER
Sarah Cramer Shields
sarahcramershields.com

EDITORIAL DIRECTOR + WRITER
Jenny Paurys
finelinesediting.com

BOOK DESIGNER
Matt Thomas, Convoy
weareconvoy.com

PROJECT MANAGER
Egidijus Paurys
finelinesediting.com

RECIPE EDITOR
Steven Blaski
finelinesediting.com

COPY EDITORS
Steven Blaski + Stephanie Goehring
finelinesediting.com + stephaniegoehring.com

PRINTER
Worth Higgins & Associates
worthhiggins.com

We are especially grateful to our husbands, families, and friends, who make it possible for us to do what we love. Thank you.